CHESAPEAKE BAY BLUES

Rob,

Thank you for the support and your hard work.

Howard

AMERICAN POLITICAL CHALLENGES
Larry J. Sabato
Series Editor

The American political process is in trouble. Although we witnessed a movement toward specific electoral reforms in the aftermath of the 2000 election debacle, the health of our political system is still at risk. Recent events have altered the political landscape and posed new challenges, and reforms are much needed and wanted by the American public. Diligence is required, however, in examining carefully the intended and unintended consequences of reforms as we look toward the 2004 elections and beyond.

Series Editor Larry J. Sabato of the University of Virginia Center for Politics is a leading political scientist and commentator who has clear ideas about what needs to change to improve the quality of our democracy. For this series, he taps leading political authors to write cogent diagnoses and prescriptions for improving both politics and government. New and forthcoming books in the series are short, to the point, easy to understand (if difficult to implement against the political grain). They take a stand and show how to overcome obstacles to change. Authors are known for their clear writing style as well as for their political acumen.

Titles in the Series

Chesapeake Bay Blues
Science, Politics, and the Struggle to Save the Bay
  Howard R. Ernst

Forthcoming

The Presidential Nominating Process
A Place for Us?
  Rhodes Cook

The Pursuit of Happiness in Times of War
  Carl M. Cannon

CHESAPEAKE BAY BLUES

SCIENCE, POLITICS, AND THE STRUGGLE TO SAVE THE BAY

HOWARD R. ERNST

ROWMAN & LITTLEFIELD PUBLISHERS, INC.
Lanham • Boulder • New York • Oxford

ROWMAN & LITTLEFIELD PUBLISHERS, INC.

Published in the United States of America
by Rowman & Littlefield Publishers, Inc.
A Member of the Rowman & Littlefield Publishing Group
4501 Forbes Boulevard, Suite 200, Lanham, Maryland 20706
www.rowmanlittlefield.com

PO Box 317, Oxford, OX2 9RU, UK

British Library Cataloguing in Publication Information Available

Library of Congress Cataloging-in-Publication Data
Ernst, Howard R., 1970–
  Chesapeake Bay blues : science, politics, and the struggle to save the
bay / Howard R. Ernst.
      p. cm.—(American political challenges)
Includes bibliographical references (p.).
  ISBN 0-7425-2350-0 (cloth : alk. paper)—ISBN 0-7425-2351-9 (pbk. :
alk. paper)
  1. Restoration ecology—Political aspects—Chesapeake Bay (Md. and
Va.) 2. Ecosystem management—Government policy—Chesapeake Bay (Md.
and Va.) 3. Blue crab—Chesapeake Bay (Md. and Va.) I. Title. II.
Series.
  QH104.5.C45 E76 2003
  333.95'616'0916347—dc21

                                                              2002152300

Printed in the United States of America

♾™ The paper used in this publication meets the minimum requirements of
American National Standard for Information Sciences—Permanence of Paper for
Printed Library Materials, ANSI/NISO Z39.48-1992.

To the memory of David Dupont
and the future of Simon Ernst

Contents

Contents

Acknowledgments

The work presented in this book benefited from numerous sources and was supported by the assistance of many generous individuals. I would like to offer thanks to leaders in the scientific community who fielded my countless questions and offered valuable comments, especially Rich Batiuk, Donald F. Boesch, Jack Greer, Carlton Haywood, Mike Hirshfield, Douglas Lipton, and Thomas W. Simpson. I owe a debt to Ann Swanson of the Chesapeake Bay Commission, who generously shared her time and political expertise. I would also like to thank the members of the Chesapeake Bay Commission who provided me with unlimited access to their meetings. Tom Horton and former Maryland Governor Harry Hughes offered their candid thoughts and served as rich sources of inspiration for this study. The staff of the Chesapeake Bay Foundation provided unique insights, especially those of Lonnie Moore, Charles Parks, Mike Shultz, and Denise Stranko. Betty Duty and Mary Madison of the Maryland Watermen's Association answered my questions and provided valuable information. Barbara MacLeod and Ceil Petro at the Maryland Department of Natural Resources Carter Library also provided useful research assistance. Melissa Stango and Joan Humenick skillfully edited the manuscript. I am also grateful to several students for assisting with my research, including Ryan Casey, Richard Ferrari, Bradley Harrison, Victor Lange, and my fall 2001 Research Methods class. I would like to thank the Naval Academy Research Council for funding this study and Jennifer Knerr of Rowman & Littlefield for recognizing the importance of this topic. My good friends at University of

Virginia's Center for Politics, Larry Sabato, Alex Theodoridis, and Joshua Scott, provided invaluable guidance and support. My colleagues at the Naval Academy, especially Douglas Brattabo, Rebecca Bill Chavez, Ian Facey, Steven Frantzich, Christine Jamison, Karen Lambert, Arthur Rachwald, and David Weiden, each supported this project in important ways. Most important, I would like to thank Tracey Ernst for her editorial assistance, sound judgment, infinite patience, and generous spirit.

Tables and Figures

TABLES

FIGURES

Introduction

Long before the first Earth Day in 1970, before the term *ecology* was coined in 1866,[1] before *green* came to represent a political symbol, even before England's North American colonies united as a nation, there existed an environmental ethic among the European settlers of the New World.[2] The dream of open spaces and abundant wildlife, as well as the opportunities that these resources represented, was a driving force behind the settlement of North America. Early evidence of the prominent role assigned to natural resources can be found throughout the colonial record, such as William Penn's 1681 decree requiring that for every five acres of land cleared in Pennsylvania, one acre was to be left in its natural state. Massachusetts, Connecticut, and New York each passed laws protecting wild game by the early eighteenth century.[3] These laws and others like them reflect the importance of the natural world in North America, which was to both attract and sustain European settlers.

By the mid-nineteenth century, America's environmental tradition had taken root and was increasingly reflected in the literature of the day. Thoreau's *Walden* (1845), like Emerson's "Nature" (1836) and Marsh's *Man and Nature* (1864), offered unprecedented reverence to the concept of nature, helping to give form to the nation's growing environmental ethic. The nineteenth century was also a period in which ecologically oriented magazines, such as *Forest and Stream* in 1873, were growing in popularity. The common theme running throughout these works was the level to which they elevated nature. They rejected the notion of nature as merely a symbol of untapped potential to be conquered and tamed. Instead, they presented nature as an end in itself, something worthy of protection regardless of its economic value.

The country's appreciation for the natural world continued to develop into the twentieth century. John Muir's *The Mountains of California* (1894) and Aldo Leopold's *Sand County Almanac* (1949) epitomize the nation's growing ecological interest. In the opening passage of his *Sand County Almanac,* Leopold writes, "There are those who can live without wild things, and some who cannot. These essays are the delights and dilemmas of one who cannot." In his simple, elegant manner, Leopold expresses his enthusiasm for nature and captures a worldview that has come to embody modern environmentalism.

The nation's environmental sentiment became increasingly reflected in government action. In 1872, the nation celebrated its first Arbor Day, and that same year Yellowstone National Park was established as the country's first natural preserve. By 1900, four additional national parks had been created—Sequoia (1890), Kings Canyon (1890), Yosemite (1890), and Mount Rainier (1899). As early as the mid-1800s, the Maryland General Assembly had passed legislation to protect its water supply—making it illegal to "throw dead animals" into the Potomac.[4] The federal government entered the environmental regulatory business for the first time in 1899 when it passed the Refuse Act of 1899, requiring individuals to obtain permits from the Army Corps of Engineers before dumping refuse into the nation's navigable waters. While in practice these measures did little to protect the nation's waterways, they do reveal the public's early concern for natural resources and willingness to take collective action to protect natural areas.

But America's environmental woes are at least as old as its environmental ethic. Open sewers, animal waste, contaminated drinking water, and the general stench of crowded cities can be traced to the seventeenth century. As early as 1652, a scarcity of clean water led the colonial city of Boston to develop the nation's first public water system. By 1800, seventeen additional cities had followed Boston's lead and established public water systems.[5] The Maryland General Assembly authorized the creation of Baltimore's water system in 1808. Moreover, it was the loss of natural resources that led to the seventeenth-century environmental decree by William Penn and the wild game protections previously mentioned. Likewise, it was pollution that led to the federal Refuse Act of 1899, and it was the loss of open spaces that led to the creation of the nation's park system in the late 1800s.

As early as the nineteenth century, the forces of industrialization and population growth had combined to hasten environmental degradation in many parts of the nation. Several cities in the United States, such as New York, Chicago, San Francisco, and Los Angeles, saw their populations more than double during the last three decades of the nineteenth century. Environmental scholar Jacqueline Switzer (1994) describes the situation at the end of the nineteenth century this way: "By 1880, New York had 287 foundries and machine shops, and another 125 steam engines, bone mills, refineries, and tanneries. By the turn of the century, Pittsburgh had hundreds of iron and steel plants, and Chicago's stockyard stench combined with eight railroads and a busy port to produce odors and thick, black smoke" (5–6).

These problems were not restricted to America's northern cities, but were increasingly evident in the Chesapeake Bay region. For example, by the mid-1850s, Baltimore was the third largest city in the United States with a population greater than 170,000. Despite its growing population, Baltimore did not develop what we would consider a modern sewage treatment system until the 1900s, leading its harbor to be described by one observer as "among the greatest stenches of the world."[6] By the end of the nineteenth century, fifteen thousand homes emptied raw sewage directly into Baltimore's Jones Falls waterway.[7]

America's environmental conflict—that is, the conflict between the nation's appreciation for the natural world and the country's deteriorating natural condition—had come into focus by the early twentieth century. Cheap fossil fuels, industrialization, and an ever-growing and consuming human population accelerated the nation's environmental decline, causing extraordinary stresses on natural systems. All the while, America's environmental ethic continued to flourish. The memberships of environmental groups, such as the Sierra Club and the Audubon Society, grew throughout the early twentieth century, providing an organizational force behind America's environmental sentiment.[8] By mid-century, it appeared that the country's environmental ethic was on a collision course with its rapidly deteriorating natural conditions.

When Rachel Carson published her classic work in 1962, *Silent Spring,* the nation was primed for her message. The country as a whole had never been more environmentally conscious, and the nation's overall environmental condition had never been worse. Carson's work, a powerful description of spring without the sounds of nature, helped to give direction to a new breed of environmentalism in America. Like her environmental predecessors, Carson expressed a profound appreciation of the natural world. What distinguished her from many earlier environmental writers was her recognition that America's growing environmental problems required political responses. Subsequent works by Lynton Caldwell (1963), Garrett Hardin (1968), Paul Ehrlich (1968), and Barry Commoner (1971) continued to direct the environmental movement in a political direction. Hardin (1968) in particular emphasized political factors, arguing that the coercive force of government was essential to successfully protect the nation's fragile environment from destructive economic forces. He wrote that economic freedoms, as they were being exercised in the mid-twentieth century, left society "free only to bring on universal ruin." Hardin believed, "Once [people] see the necessity of mutual coercion, they become free to pursue other goals" (1248). His work, unlike the works of so many of his predecessors, was not primarily intended to raise the nation's environmental awareness; Hardin's work united political, economic, and environmental ideas in a call to action.

STRESSING POLITICS

Recent scholarship has continued to emphasize the government's central role in protecting the environment. Vig and Kraft (1997) explain the logic behind this position, "The government plays a preeminent role in this policy area because most environmental threats represent public or collective goods problems. They cannot be solved through purely private actions" (3). Thinkers like these argue that economic markets, driven by the forces of competition and profit, are ill equipped to protect environmental conditions.

Economists and political scientists often refer to the unintended and unwanted by-products of production as "externalities."[9] Externalities come in any number of forms. For example, a developer who builds a new shopping center not only provides additional shopping space to the community, but also increases the amount of sediments entering nearby streams and reduces the availability of natural habitat for local wildlife. Likewise, fertilizers applied by commercial farmers produce water pollution as well as more bountiful crops. And industrial production that transforms raw materials into useful products is also likely to discharge pollutants into the air and water.

With goals of limiting the by-products of industrial society and preserving the environment, substantial government programs were established in the 1970s.[10] Most notably, the Environmental Protection Agency (EPA) was created by executive order in 1970, providing environmental interests a permanent place at the nation's public policy table.[11] The EPA quickly became the nation's largest regulatory agency. By the end of the 1970s, its annual budget had grown to over $1 billion, and the agency maintained a professional staff of more than ten thousand people.[12] Two of the most notable legislative accomplishments of this time included the Clean Air Act (1970) and the Water Pollution Control Act (1972), which was passed over a presidential veto. These acts imposed federally mandated environmental standards on the states, helping to transform the federal government's role in environmental protection.[13]

Since the 1970s, environmental politics has become an institutionalized part of America's political life at every level of government. Local, state, and federal governmental bodies continuously face problems that have important environmental consequences. At the federal level, Congress has more than a dozen committees and thirty-one subcommittees that have jurisdiction over EPA actions,[14] while state governments control their own regulatory and oversight bodies.[15] The courts have also become increasingly important in the area of environmental protection, with regulatory measures frequently being challenged through the legal system. Add to this the complexity of understanding the interest group context in which environmental politics unfolds and fluctuations in public opinion regarding environmental matters, and one begins to appreciate the conceptual maze that comprises modern environmental politics.

This study builds from the central idea that the political process is ultimately responsible for preventing environmental degradation in this country. It is not industry, development, or the nation's growing population that poses the greatest threat to the environment; it is shortcomings within the political process that perpetuate environmental degradation, and it is the political process that holds the key to restoring the nation's environmental condition. Achieving the types of regulatory controls, economic incentives, fiscal resources, and scientific innovations that are necessary to achieve and maintain a healthy environment (i.e., limit externalities to an acceptable level) is only possible through collective action. With this in mind, this book asks the central question: *why has governmental action not been more successful in restoring precious ecosystems like the Chesapeake Bay?*

ORGANIZATIONAL STRUCTURE OF THE BOOK

This study addresses environmental politics by focusing on the political life of a single ecosystem—the Chesapeake Bay. By narrowing the analysis to one ecosystem, rather than addressing environmental politics in general or a broad subset of environmental issues (e.g., watershed politics), the work is free to delve deeply into the complex political and ecological forces that influence environmental policy.[16] While the case and its findings are specific to the Chesapeake Bay, the nearly century-long political struggle to protect the Bay and its resources is echoed in other environmental clashes across the country. Whether the struggle is to save the Florida Everglades, California's Sequoias, the San Francisco Bay, or the Great Lakes,[17] the roadblocks to successful political action are all too familiar.

In the first section of the book, chapter 1 outlines the environmental condition of the Chesapeake Bay and discusses political actions that have been taken to restore the ecosystem. The chapter reveals that despite widespread public concern and over two decades of political attention, the Chesapeake Bay remains in dreadfully poor condition. Chapter 2 lays out the study's environmental policy theory, offering a political explanation of the complex forces that have impeded the environmental restoration of the Chesapeake Bay.

In part II of the book, the first case study is explored. Chapter 3 introduces the issue of nutrient waste, the Bay's single greatest pollution problem. Chapter 4 explores the politics behind nutrient management by applying the study's environmental theory to agricultural nutrient controls in Pennsylvania and Maryland.

The third part includes chapters 5 and 6, which follow a similar pattern as the two preceding chapters. Here, the ecological and political factors influencing blue crab management are explored.

The final section of the book, chapter 7, applies the lessons of the study to the Bay's environmental future, suggesting ten political steps that could be taken to help improve the environmental quality of this valuable natural resource.

Part I

THE CHESAPEAKE BAY AND ENVIRONMENTAL POLITICS

1

The Chesapeake Bay

Management of North America's Largest Estuary

Frankly, I would have hoped that it [Chesapeake Bay restoration] would have been further along than it is after 18 years.

—Harry Hughes (2002), governor of Maryland from 1979 to 1987

It has been said that it is the best restoration program around the country. I was once the best track runner in my high school—it was a small school, and I was really slow.

—Mike Shultz (2002), Chesapeake Bay Foundation

The Chesapeake Bay is a unique and dynamic ecosystem. The geological forces responsible for shaping the Bay can be traced back some 18,000 years when glacial melting marked the end of the last ice age (Pleistocene period) and triggered a rise in sea level that eventually flooded the Susquehanna River valley and formed the Chesapeake Bay.[1] Fossil records reveal that as recently as 12,000 years ago mammoths, mastodons, bison, and caribou roamed the area that comprises the Chesapeake watershed.[2] North American Indians, the first human inhabitants in the region, are believed to have occupied the area as early as 11,000 years ago, roughly 8,000 years before the Bay reached its current size and shape.[3]

Today the Bay and its tributaries cover more than 4,500 square miles, or 41 million acres, and are estimated to include 18 trillion gallons of water.[4] Nearly 200 miles long and 35 miles wide at its widest point,[5] it is one of North America's largest bodies of water. Including tidal tributaries, the Bay contains approximately 11,700 miles of shore-line. Roughly half of the Bay's water is supplied from the 150 rivers, streams, and creeks that flow into it, draining a mammoth 64,000-square-mile watershed that spans six states—Delaware, Maryland, New York, Pennsylvania, Virginia, and West Virginia. The remainder of the Bay's water comes from the Atlantic Ocean. Despite its massive pro-portions, the Bay is a relatively shallow body of water, averaging only 21 feet.[6] The Environmental Protection Agency claims that a person six feet tall could wade across 700,000 acres of the Bay without becoming submerged.[7]

The Chesapeake Bay is the largest of the nation's 850 estuaries. The word *estuary*, derived from the Latin root *aestus* (tide), is defined as "a semienclosed coastal body of water that has a measurable salinity gradient from its freshwater drainage to its ocean entrance."[8] It is a place where freshwater and saltwater meet in a continuous and turbu-lent process. Open to the ocean, coastal tides provide the Bay with a twice-daily surge of saltwater. Fed by numerous freshwater streams and rivers, the largest being Pennsylvania's Susquehanna River,[9] the Bay is influenced by rain and snowfall throughout the watershed. Conse-quently, the salinity of the Bay is in constant flux, depending on the daily tides, lunar phases, and weather conditions throughout the re-gion.[10] The salinity also varies substantially at different depths, or zones, with lighter freshwater found toward the surface and heavier saltwater toward the bottom. These salinity zones often flow in oppo-site directions, with freshwater from rivers and streams flowing south toward the ocean, and heavier saltwater from the Atlantic pushing north with each tide.[11]

Until recently, the shallow waters and marshy banks of this giant estuary served as an ideal habitat for roughly three thousand migratory and resident species. Historically, the Chesapeake Bay has been the most productive bay in North America. The fecundity of the Bay led the Al-gonquin Indians to name it "Chesepiooc," the great shellfish bay;[12] more recent observers have described the Bay as "an immense protein factory."[13] Throughout much of the early twentieth century, the Bay's oyster harvest was so bountiful that an average of thirteen railroad cars a day left Baltimore Harbor loaded with oysters, hauling annual Bay harvests that regularly exceeded thirty million pounds. The Bay's first fisheries survey, conducted in 1880, recorded 123 million pounds of oysters harvested from the Bay in that year alone.[14] The oysters were not alone in their prodigious numbers. The Bay once provided a home for immense populations of blue crabs, ducks, striped bass, shad, herring, and other natural treasures that far exceeded current levels. Even today, the Bay sustains a commercial harvest that has a net worth of over $1 billion per year.

For those familiar with the current state of the Bay, it is difficult to comprehend the natural richness this unique ecosystem once supported. The Bay that has been lost was an ecosystem with clear water that supported extensive fields of underwater grasses, as much as 600,000 acres, and vast expanses of oyster beds, over 400,000 acres.[15] It was an ecosystem that sustained massive populations of fish and wildlife. Fish species such as the American shad and sturgeon, unfamiliar to many residents of the Bay today, were once two of the Bay's most abundant species. In the 1930s, the American shad supported the second most important commercial fishery in the Bay, second only to the oyster fishery, with annual harvests exceeding nine million pounds.[16] Who today can fathom the Bay watershed as an unspoiled area that provided a single hunting party in 1760 with 111 bison, 18 black bear, 114 bobcats, 98 deer, 2 elk, 112 foxes, 109 gray wolves, 41 mountain lions, and 500 unidentified mammals?[17] While the natural Bay, the near Eden described in the notes of Thomas Hariot in 1588, Robert Beverly in 1705, and William Bird in 1737,[18] is likely gone forever, the question remains, what is left of this natural treasure and what can be done to protect it for the future?

MANAGING THE CHESAPEAKE BAY

Given the size and importance of this ecosystem, it is not surprising that its health has received a great deal of public and political attention.[19] As early as the late nineteenth century, state fishery boards were established in Maryland and Virginia to help manage the Bay's limited resources. Poor water quality, overharvesting, and disease took a heavy toll on the Bay's fisheries throughout the mid- and late twentieth century. The first attempt at bistate resource management for the Bay occurred in 1924 when the governors of Maryland and Virginia met to discuss the management needs of the Bay's blue crab population.[20] Though the meeting failed to produce a common management strategy for the crab, a goal that has yet to be achieved, it did successfully highlight the need for a common regulatory approach for the Bay's many migratory species.

The first regional conference to address the Bay's overall health and management needs was held in Baltimore in 1933.[21] At this conference representatives from the federal government (U.S. Bureau of Fisheries), Virginia, the District of Columbia, Maryland, and Delaware discussed the Bay's growing environmental problems. The opening remarks of Dr. Thomas Cullen, a well-respected surgeon and member of the Johns Hopkins Medical School who chaired the 1933 conference, summarizes the purpose of the historic meeting:

> We have been working on this matter of the Chesapeake Bay for a long time, everybody has been interested in it for many years. . . . The people of Virginia have their interests, those of Maryland have their interests, those in Delaware have their interests, and the same is true with respect to Washington and Pennsylvania. . . . We believe there is a decided advantage to be gained by all of us getting together and looking at Chesapeake Bay, first, as it is now, taking stock of what has been done, then giving further consideration as to what can be done.[22]

The participants at this early conference had a surprisingly sophisticated understanding of the numerous problems and management needs facing the Chesapeake Bay. Conference participants focused on such diverse issues as the negative consequences of inadequate sewage treatment, the health consequences of pollution, the effects of overharvesting the Bay's living resources (oysters and crabs in particular), and the problem of soil erosion—issues that continue to plague the restoration effort to this day. In particular, the participants were aware of the need for a common management approach for the Bay's collective problems. Swepson Earle, the Maryland state conservation commissioner at the time, explained his desire for a Baywide management strategy:

> Wipeout this imaginary line across Chesapeake Bay that divides Maryland and Virginia. It is impossible to place a wall along the line and say, "Crabs, stay down in Virginia," and "Fish, stay up in Maryland," because these things that God has given us for Chesapeake Bay, these things that are migratory like crabs and fish, must go to other waters in the Bay in order that they develop and become mature, and it can only be done by wise use, constructive measures, and no feeling of jealousy between the two states.[23]

The conference produced several suggestions for the creation of a permanent Chesapeake Bay committee to help coordinate and promote the preservation effort. On the final day of the conference, participants unanimously agreed to create a multistate committee with representatives from Virginia, Maryland, Delaware, the District of Columbia, and possibly Pennsylvania. They envisioned a small central committee with an equal number of representatives from each state that would be appointed by the various state governors and would oversee the activities of several subcommittees. The subcommittees were to be organized around specific Bay issues, such as health, sanitation, and conservation.[24] Unfortunately, the permanent, multistate committee proposed at the 1933 conference did not materialize, and Bay protection remained primarily an uncoordinated activity in the years following the conference.

The second major push for Baywide management took place in 1965, when legislation was passed through the River and Harbor Act of 1965 that provided the U.S. Army Corps of Engineers with funding to complete the first comprehensive analysis of present and future conditions of the Chesapeake Bay. The program evolved into a $15 million study that coordinated the research efforts of federal, state, and local agencies, as well as several scientific institutions.[25] The study was organized around three primary objectives:

1. Assess the existing physical, chemical, biological, economic, and environmental conditions of Chesapeake Bay and its water resources.
2. Project the future water resource needs of Chesapeake Bay to the year 2020.
3. Formulate and recommend solutions to problems using the Chesapeake Bay Hydraulic Model.

In fulfillment of its first goal, the Corps produced a seven-volume report in 1973 that provided an unprecedented account of the existing state of the Chesapeake Bay and its resources. Three years later, in April 1976, the Corps' hydraulic model of the Bay, an enclosed, nine-acre replica of the Chesapeake Bay region, was completed.[26] Following completion of the Hydraulic Model, the Corps released its *Chesapeake Bay Future Conditions Report* in 1977. This twelve-volume report satisfied the project's second major goal of estimating the state of the Bay and its resources to the year 2020. The purpose of the study was to identify problems and conflicts that threaten the future health of the Bay so that policymakers could move toward the third and final stage of the program, the plan-formulation stage.

Unfortunately, the plan-formulation stage, the stage in which the scientific findings were to be applied to Baywide management, was not realized. Instead, in 1976, Congress funded a second comprehensive study of the Bay, this time to be carried out under the direction of the Environmental Protection Agency (EPA). Like the Corps of Engineers study before it, the EPA's seven-year, $27 million study found substantial deterioration of the Chesapeake Bay and called for government action to protect the endangered ecosystem. Since 1976, the EPA has become the lead agency in the ongoing restoration effort, working in partnership with federal, regional, state, and local programs in what is often touted as the nation's premier environmental-monitoring and restoration program.

The restoration effort's political structure began to take shape in 1980 when policymakers in Virginia and Maryland came together to establish the Chesapeake Bay Commission.[27] Pennsylvania, which has a major influence on water quality in the Bay, joined the Commission in 1985. While the Commission has no regulatory authority, it serves in an advisory capacity to the legislative assemblies of the three states and as a liaison to the U.S. Congress, offering advice and recommendations to the legislative bodies. Today, the Commission maintains a central office in Annapolis and satellite offices in Virginia and Pennsylvania. The Commission comprises twenty-one members. Each state is represented by five state legislators, their director of natural resources, and one citizen representative. The executive director of the Commission represents all three states.

Another major move toward restoration occurred in 1983 when the EPA issued the findings from its Baywide study. On December 9 of that year, the governors of Maryland, Virginia, Pennsylvania; the mayor of the District of Columbia; the administrator of the EPA, and the chair of the Chesapeake Bay Commission signed the first Chesapeake Bay Agreement. The initial Bay Agreement, little more than a paragraph in length, expressed a desire by the signatories to improve the Bay. The stated goals of the 1983 Chesapeake Bay Agreement were to "implement coordinated plans to improve and protect water quality and living resources of the Chesapeake Bay estuarine system."[28] This Agreement established a unique tristate partnership that recognized the regional importance of the Bay and the substantial problems associated with establishing environmental policy for an area that spans a diverse geographic and political area.

Since the 1983 Agreement, there have been two additional Bay Agreements—one in 1987 and one in 2000.[29] The more recent Agreements are much more detailed and substantive than the original, laying out specific goals for Bay restoration and strategies for achieving success. The 1987 Agreement established 31 formal commitments (i.e., goals) and the 2000 Agreement established 105 commitments. The 2000 Agreement, by far the most ambitious of the Agreements, spans thirteen pages and addresses five separate areas of Bay restoration: (1) living resources, (2) habitat restoration, (3) water quality, (4) land use, and (5) community engagement. While each Agreement has grown in specificity, the overall goal of the Agreements remains the same—the restoration and protection of the Bay's water quality and living resources.[30]

The initial Bay Agreement led to the creation of the Chesapeake Bay Program, an Environmental Protection Agency–funded program governed by an executive council consisting of the six signatories of the Bay Agreement. The Bay Program serves as the implementation arm of the Bay Agreements. Beyond the executive council, the program is divided into implementation committees and eight subcommittees (see figure 1.1). The committees cover the full gamut of the Bay's environmental problems. Though it took fifty years to come to fruition, the Bay Program, with its multistate representation, small executive council, and numerous subcommittees organized around specific Bay issues, embodies the type of permanent Chesapeake Bay committee proposed at the original 1933 Chesapeake Bay conference.

Since its inception, the Bay Program has been awarded more than $282 million in federal funds (1984–2002), most of which it allocates to the states and other organizations as grants to fund restoration programs for the Bay.[31] For the 2002 fiscal year alone, the Bay Program was allocated $19.5 million. That year, the federal government also funded several additional programs designed to address specific aspects of the restoration effort. For instance, during the 2002 fiscal year, the federal government granted $1.75 million to the Small Watershed Program, $2.75 million for the National Oceanic and Atmospheric Administration (NOAA) Chesapeake Bay Program Office, $1.2 million for

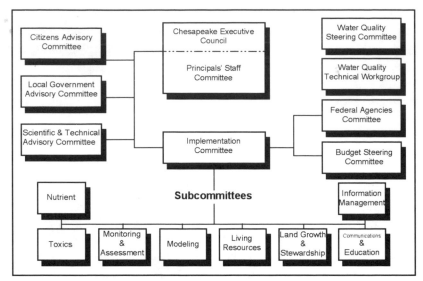

Figure 1.1. Chesapeake Bay Program Organizational Structure
Source: **Created by Christine Jamison from Chesapeake Bay Program (2002b).**

NOAA's Chesapeake Bay Education Program, $3 million to the Corps of Engineers' oyster replenishment programs, $2 million for the NOAA Sea Grant Oyster Disease Program, $1.2 million to the National Park Service's Chesapeake Bay programs, $18.2 million to continue phase II of the Poplar Island Beneficial Use of Dredging Material Project, and $6 million to the Natural Resources Conservation Service.[32] All told, federal funding totaled more than $55 million in 2002.

Federal funding represents only one aspect of the overall spending equation. Each year, the individual states also commit substantial resources to support the restoration effort. The exact amount states spend on Bay programs is difficult to calculate, since many state programs are at least partially funded by federal grants, which creates a funding overlap. State programs that influence the Bay may also apply to areas beyond the Chesapeake Bay watershed or only indirectly relate to the restoration effort. In 2002, the Maryland Department of Natural Resources attempted to estimate the total amount Maryland spends on Bay-related programs. The analysis found that Maryland, a state that has been generous in allocating resources for the Bay, is on track to spend an average of $630 million a year for Bay programs in the coming years.[33] Though Maryland's partner states are unlikely to approach this level of spending, Maryland's spending combined with federal spending illustrates the enormity of the existing effort to restore the Chesapeake Bay.[34]

While the current funding level is impressive and a true testament to the century-long political struggle to secure funding for the Bay, the available resources pale in comparison to what has been estimated to be necessary to successfully offset three hundred years of environmental exploitation and neglect. According to an analysis conducted by the Chesapeake Bay Foundation, a well-respected nonprofit organization working to improve the Bay since 1967, it will cost a minimum of $8.5 billion to meet the water quality and land use goals outlined in the latest Chesapeake Bay Agreement by the 2010 deadline.[35] More recent estimates, based on figures from Maryland officials, place the overall cost of protecting the Bay closer to $20 billion, with Virginia spending close to $9 billion, Maryland spending $7 billion, and Pennsylvania and the District of Columbia contributing roughly $4 billion by the year 2010.[36] It is clear to most observers of the restoration program that if funding continues at current levels, it will fall billions of dollars short of what is needed to meet the stated goals.

The public effort to restore the Bay is even less impressive when compared to the private development that is taking place in the Bay's watershed. From 1950 to 2000, the population in the watershed nearly doubled, from roughly 8 million to 15 million people. Conservative estimates place the number at 18 million by the year 2020.[37] Population growth in turn leads to additional sewage, pollution, waste, and the loss of natural lands—all of which adversely impact the health of the Bay. According to Debbie Osborne, director of the Trust for Public Land's Chesapeake Field Office, 128,000 acres a year are lost to development and sprawl throughout the watershed.[38] Add to this the pressure caused by the industrialization of agribusiness, the increased efficiency of commercial fishing, and air pollution caused by the influx of automobiles and motorboats in the area, and one begins to appreciate the difficulty of restoring the Bay without aggressive environmental planning and funding.

The net result is what two environmental analysts explain as a situation in which progress is a bit like "rowing ahead at four knots when the current is moving against us at five knots."[39] Environmental advocates are left with the hollow satisfaction that things may have been worse had no action been taken, but they are unable to establish that past or current levels of action have resulted in a sustained overall improvement in the health of the ecosystem. Faced with mounting pressures, simply holding the line, maintaining the Bay at a severely depleted level, all too often passes for "success."

The inventory of living resources that follows suggests that the overall effort to restore the Chesapeake Bay has been far from successful. Quite simply, the Bay is a huge ecosystem demanding an equally large effort to successfully protect it from the onslaught of development and pollution that modern life presents. While it is easy to get lost in figures and to judge the governmental action by the number of agreements it produces or the amount of money that is spent on restoration, the ultimate measures of progress are the Bay's living resources. With this in mind, the following section assesses the success of restoration efforts to date by exploring recent trends in the vitality of the Bay's living resources.[40]

THE STATE OF THE BAY:
A LIMITED INVENTORY OF LIVING RESOURCES

We ride in a thicket. We grapple with difficulties; we are in a maze of routine. Letters, circulars, reports, and special cases beset our paths as the logs, gullies, rocks, and bog-holes and mosquitoes beset us in the hills. We ride—but are we getting anywhere?

—Aldo Leopold (1913), "To the Forest Officers of the Carson"

In his 1913 letter to the forest officers of Carson National Forest in New Mexico, renowned forester and naturalist, Aldo Leopold, ponders, "What is the best way to measure the success of conservation efforts?" Leopold concluded that the health of the ecosystem, not the amount spent or the number of studies conducted, is the ultimate measure of environmental management success. He argued that environmental studies and restoration programs are at best a means to an end (i.e., a healthy ecosystem) and should be evaluated by the extent to which they bring about that end.

Recently, public policy analysts have questioned whether changes to environmental conditions are the single best method for measuring environmental management success. Leach and associates, for example, argue that success should be measured in a wide range of areas, including building future capacity, education efforts, creating collaborative agreements, resolving conflict, monitoring programs, and policy change.[41] However, even the Leach et al. study concludes that the long-term success of a restoration program must ultimately be measured by the "partnership's impacts on physical, biological, or social aspects of watershed-related problems."[42] The Chesapeake Bay Commission also acknowledges that restoration success should be measured in terms of ecological conditions.[43]

Since the partnership to restore the Bay has been in place for an extended period of time and hundreds of millions of dollars have been spent over this period toward Bay restoration, it makes sense that environmental indicators are the most meaningful measures of the success for this particular ecosystem. While this may not be true for restoration programs that have been in place for only a few years, since programs may take a number of years to be fully implemented and may have multiyear lag times before they translate into environmental improvements, the long-standing history of the Bay restoration effort minimizes these concerns.

It is therefore appropriate to apply Leopold's central question to the Chesapeake Bay, "Are we getting anywhere?" What has been the impact of the nearly thirty-year effort to improve the environmental health of the Bay? In this section, several key Bay resources (i.e., oysters, aquatic grasses, blue crabs, striped bass, shad, and alewife) are tracked. These resources were chosen because of their importance to the Bay, the amount of attention they have received from other studies, and because of the substantial amount of resources that have been dedicated toward restoring these living resources. Logic suggests that resources that have received the greatest amount of restoration attention should have improved the most in recent years.

Oysters

The oyster population has long served as both an important commercial resource for Bay fishermen and as a valuable filter of the Bay's water. Unfortunately, the health of the Chesapeake Bay oyster population has been on the decline for at least the last fifty years. In the early 1950s, it was not unusual for annual oyster harvests to exceed 35 million pounds. As late as the early 1980s, annual harvests of 20 million pounds were recorded. By the mid-1990s, however, the deteriorating condition of the Bay, disease, and poor management practices led to the collapse of the oyster population.[44] The decline is illustrated most clearly by the diminishing annual harvests outlined in figure 1.2. Recent

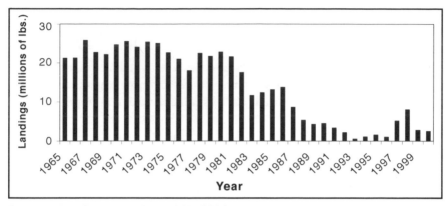

Figure 1.2. Oyster Landing 1965–2000
Source: **Compiled by author from National Marine Fisheries Service (2001).**

harvests have produced less than 600,000 pounds of oysters, a dramatic 98 percent reduction since the mid-1950s.[45]

Beyond the economic effect of reduced harvests, the reduction in the Bay's oyster stock has important environmental consequences.[46] It has been estimated that a single oyster can filter as much as two gallons of water through its gills in an hour. The filtering process enables oysters to remove sediments from the water and deposit them as waste on the bottom of the Bay, thereby providing clearer water for the Bay's other resources. Moreover, the hard shells of oysters combine to form large formations known as beds. These beds, when healthy and abundant, provide protection and habitat for other Bay creatures.[47]

Aquatic Grasses

Aquatic grasses are considered an important measuring stick of the overall quality of the Bay's water. Since the sun's rays sustain underwater grasses, they only thrive in clear water where light is able to penetrate the water's surface.[48] Historically, the Bay's expansive shallows and relatively clear water provided an ideal setting for the growth of underwater grasses, creating massive meadows of underwater vegetation. The potential habitat for Bay grasses is estimated to be around 600,000 acres (i.e., the amount of aquatic vegetation the Bay would support if it was in full health). The actual amount of acreage covered by aquatic grasses, measured by aerial surveys, is roughly one-tenth this amount (see figure 1.3).

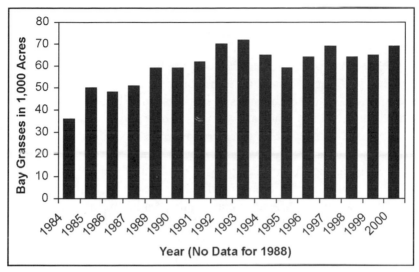

Figure 1.3. Underwater Vegetation
Source: **Maryland Department of Natural Resources (2002a).**

More than merely an indicator of water quality, the grasses, of which there are more than a dozen varieties, provide food for birds and habitat for other living resources.[49] In particular, the brant and redhead, two bird species that rely on grasses for food, have been particularly hard hit by the loss of aquatic grasses in the Bay.[50] Shrimp, crabs, seahorses, and other animals make use of the grasses as nurseries and breeding grounds. The root systems of the underwater grasses also provide environmental benefits, helping to contain the Bay's soil and reducing the harmful effects of erosion.

Blue Crabs

Perhaps no living resource symbolizes the Bay ecosystem, and the Bay's environmental problems, more than the venerable and hearty blue crab. According to the 2002 *State of the Bay Report* conducted by the Chesapeake Bay Foundation, the blue crab population stands at 42 percent of its potential, down 4 percent from the previous year.[51] Extensive studies by the National Oceanic and Atmospheric Administration's Chesapeake Bay Blue Crab Stock Assessment Committee and a host of other major research groups further illustrate the blue crab's struggle to survive in recent years. Whether one looks at the spawning female index, the annual crab harvest, crab surveys from Virginia and Maryland, or the Chesapeake Bay Foundation's estimates, a similar picture is revealed—the blue crab is not doing well in the Chesapeake Bay.[52]

Chapter 5 explores the condition of the blue crab in greater detail. It shows that while fishing pressure from commercial crabbers has increased in recent years, annual crab harvests have substantially decreased. In other words, commercial fishermen are working harder and catching fewer crabs than they have in the past. A recent report by the National Oceanic and Atmospheric Administration warned that the crab population is dangerously low and a single natural disturbance, such as a tropical storm, could lead to a collapse of the crab population.[53] These concerns have been echoed throughout the scientific community, leading to a consensus recommendation by the Bi-State Blue Crab Advisory Committee to reduce crabbing pressure by 15 percent to protect the crab from further decline.[54]

The declining numbers have primarily been attributed to intense fishing pressure, the loss of habitat provided by underwater grasses, oxygen depletion caused by nutrient pollutants entering the Bay, and natural cycles.[55] The resilience of the crab and its ability to thrive under hostile conditions make the recent downward trend particularly disconcerting. The crab has a proven ability to live in the Bay's saltiest waters as well as the Bay's freshwater tributaries. Moreover, the crab has even adapted to the highly polluted sections of the Bay including Baltimore Harbor and Norfolk's Elizabeth River.[56] The recent decline in the blue crab suggests that even one of the Bay's most robust and tenacious creatures, perhaps one of the heartiest creatures on earth, cannot withstand relentless harvesting and habitat destruction.

Fish

Two carnivorous species that have historically been of commercial and recreational importance to the Chesapeake Bay are the striped bass (commonly referred to as the rockfish) and the Atlantic croaker (also known as the hardhead). Both species dramatically decreased in numbers during the 1970s and 1980s. The Chesapeake Bay Program estimates that the decline in the striped bass population during the 1970s and 1980s led to the loss of seven thousand fishing-related jobs. In response to the decline, Maryland and Delaware placed fishing moratoriums on the striped bass from 1985 to 1989; Virginia followed with a one-year moratorium in 1989. While the recovery of the striped bass is impressive, the gains of the Atlantic croaker should be qualified. It is worth noting that in 1937 the Virginia harvest of the Atlantic croaker alone exceeded 54 million pounds, suggesting that the current rebound falls well short of this species' potential in the Chesapeake Bay. Nevertheless, in a region where environmental restoration success stories are few and far between, the rebound of striped bass and croaker provides hope for restoration efforts (see figures 1.4 and 1.5).

The story of the American shad and alewife, two filter feeders, reveals unmitigated natural resource management failures.[57] Through the early 1900s, shad were caught in larger numbers than any other fish in the Chesapeake Bay. At the beginning of the twentieth century, fishermen in the Bay reported landing more than ten million pounds of shad a year. Both the shad and the alewife were found in relatively large numbers through the 1950s, though reports of dwindling shad landings date back at least as early as the 1920s.[58] Habitat destruction, decreased water quality in the Bay, and overfishing has severely depleted these species in the Chesapeake. Despite a moratorium on fishing shad in Virginia and Maryland, an ambitious restocking effort, and an effort to open

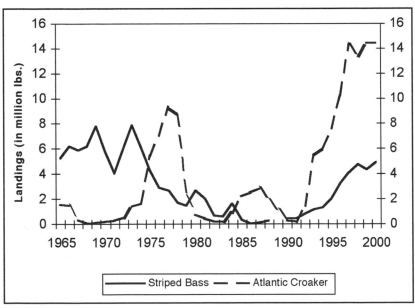

Figure 1.4. Striped Bass and Atlantic Croaker Landings 1965–2000
Source: **Compiled by author from National Marine Fisheries Service (2001).**

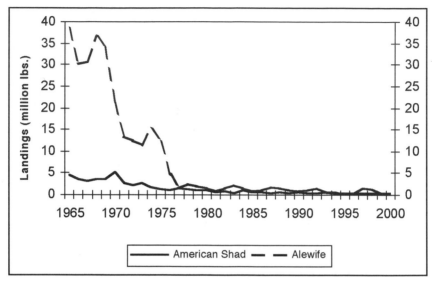

Figure 1.5. American Shad and Alewife Landings 1965–2000
Source: **Compiled by author from National Marine Fisheries Service (2001).**

rivers and streams for the passage of shad, the population has failed to recover in significant numbers.[59] Likewise, the alewife, which has received fewer protections than the shad, has also failed to experience an appreciable rebound.

It is important to note that many fish populations that have survived in the Bay are struggling with pollution-related illness and contamination. Every fish tested by the Maryland Department of the Environment in a recent survey had contaminant levels sufficient to warrant public health advisories.[60] Common contaminants included polychlorinated biphenyls (PCBs), mercury, and pesticides. Moreover, scientists now fear that over one-half of the Bay's striped bass population is infected with a progressive disease called mycobacteriosis. The chronic ailment, which has been compared to tuberculosis in humans, causes the fish to lose weight and develop potentially fatal lesions. At the present time, scientists are unsure how this widespread disease will affect the Bay's striped bass stock.

Humans

At least one of the Bay's living resources, its human population, has faired remarkably well over the last fifty years. From 1950 to the year 2000, the human population in the area has nearly doubled, increasing from just over 8 million to nearly 16 million (see figure 1.6). Not only have the numbers increased, but the life expectancy of the population, as well as the material assets of the population, has also steadily increased. Today, there are more people, living longer, consuming more resources, and producing larger quantities of waste, than at any other time in Bay history. The excesses of this adaptive and remarkably successful species are perhaps the primary environmental threat to the Bay's other living resources.

Overall Health of the Bay

No living resource exists in isolation from the overall health of the Bay. For example, human waste in the form of sewage, agricultural runoff, and atmospheric pollution can diminish water quality in the Bay and may lead to algae blooms and reduced oxygen levels in Bay waters, which in extreme forms is linked to fish kills. Algae blooms also cloud the Bay's water, thereby reducing the ability of underwater grasses to receive life-supporting sunlight. The reduction of underwater grasses, in turn, diminishes an important habitat for juvenile crabs

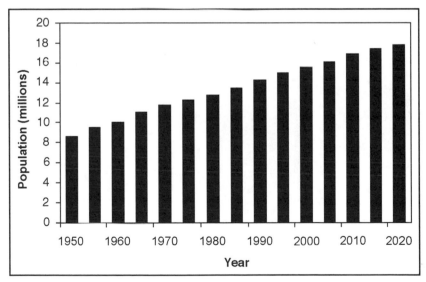

Figure 1.6.   Population Projection: Chesapeake Bay Watershed
Source: **Chesapeake Bay Program (1999c, 1).**

and an important food source for many of the Bay's birds, further stressing the ecosystem. The web of connections that comprise the overall Bay ecosystem is extremely complex and only partially understood by environmental scientists.

With these connections in mind, the Chesapeake Bay Foundation annually attempts to compile a measurement tool for the overall health of the Bay in its *State of the Bay Report*. The foundation measures the Bay's health in thirteen different areas ranging from wetlands to shad.[61] Each of the thirteen categories is scored on a 0 to 100 scale, as a measure of the actual abundance of the environmental indicator against the estimated abundance of the indicator prior to human interference. A score of 100 suggests that a resource has not been negatively affected by human influence, while a score of zero would suggest the resource had been entirely eliminated (see figure 1.7).

From these scores, the Chesapeake Bay Foundation (CBF) estimates the overall health of the Bay as a function of its natural life-supporting potential. In 2001, CBF gave the Bay an overall health score of 27, suggesting that the Bay is 73 percent less productive than

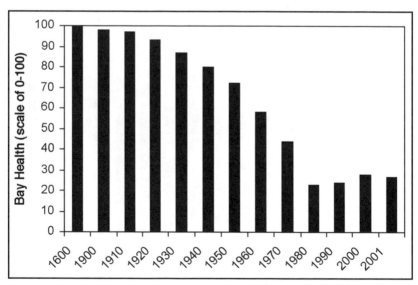

Figure 1.7.   Health of the Chesapeake Bay (1600–2001): Chesapeake Bay Foundation Index Score
Source: **Chesapeake Bay Foundation (2002a).**

it would be in a natural state and that the Bay's environmental health actually declined from the previous year. The Chesapeake Bay Foundation's scoring suggests that the Bay underwent a period of rapid deterioration between the 1950s and the 1980s. It also illustrates that the two-decade effort to restore the Bay, beginning in the 1980s, has resulted in little, if any, improvement of the overall environmental quality of the Bay. For the most part, environmental management efforts thus far have at best stalled the rapid decline of the 1970s and 1980s and have "successfully" maintained the Bay at a severely depleted level.

Looking at the total commercial fish landings in the Bay from 1950 to 2000 reveals a similar picture (see figures 1.8 and 1.9). This data, collected by the National Marine Fisheries Service, combines the total commercial landings of finfish and shellfish throughout the Chesapeake Bay. Over forty different species are included in the figures. What the numbers reveal is that despite a growing demand for fish products and advances in fishing techniques, the aggregate amount of fish taken from the Bay has declined in recent years, sug-

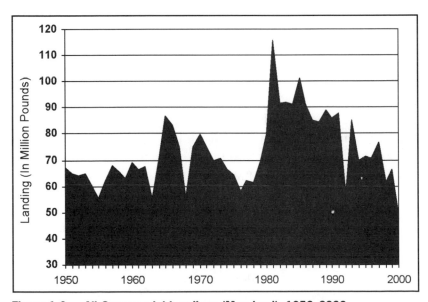

Figure 1.8. All Commercial Landings (Maryland), 1950–2000
Source: Compiled by author from National Marine Fisheries Service (2001).

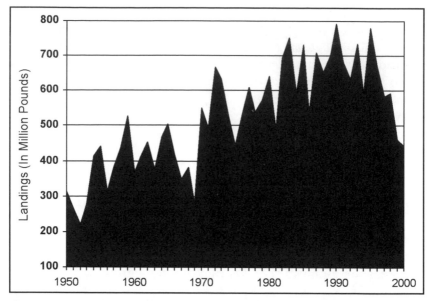

Figure 1.9. All Commercial Landings (Virginia), 1950–2000
Source: Compiled by author from National Marine Fisheries Service (2001).

gesting that the Bay's living resources are not adequately responding to restoration efforts.

CONCLUSION

Few would argue that the Chesapeake Bay as a living resource is functioning anywhere near its full potential. The vibrant bay that English explorer John Smith described in 1608 has little in common with the Chesapeake Bay of the twenty-first century. Species that once flourished in the Bay area have been entirely eliminated, while others struggle to survive at depleted levels. The effort to restore the Bay has experienced only modest success. Some species, such as the striped bass and Atlantic croaker, have returned to the Bay in large numbers, suggesting that restoration efforts, when carried out aggressively and thoughtfully, can achieve success. But for the vast majority of species, and the Bay as a whole, restoration efforts have failed to bring about the desired changes.

The remainder of this book explores the Bay's environmental problems from a political perspective, explaining how political forces often complicate and hamper the passage and implementation of environmental public policy. It addresses why the sincere concerns of the general public and the hard work of dozens of public officials and scientists have not yielded better results for the Bay. The underlying hope of this work is that a better understanding of the Bay's political life may lead to more meaningful public responses to the Bay's environmental problems.

2

The Chesapeake Bay as a Political Dilemma

Understanding the Political Barriers to Environmental Policy

Somebody is going to suffer; they have to vote in a way that hurts constituents, and that is tough.

—Richard A. Tilghman (2002), Pennsylvania state senator

On my gravestone it will say, "She held the line."

—Ann Swanson (2002), executive director
of the Chesapeake Bay Commission

The difficulty of explaining environmental politics is similar to the difficulties faced by those studying ecological systems; both endeavors attempt to provide meaningful explanations to complex, dynamic processes. Both undertakings attempt to bring conceptual order to what on the surface appears to be a chaotic network of relationships that defy explanation. To begin to understand an ecosystem, it is not only necessary to have knowledge about each species within the system, it is also necessary to appreciate how the species interact with each other and with the overall system—a difficult task indeed. Likewise, to come to terms with environmental politics, it is necessary to develop an understanding of the forces that drive environmental public policy and to comprehend how these forces influence each other, as well as the overall policy process.

The challenge is to develop a conceptual framework, a theory, for environmental politics that reduces the process to a manageable conceptual level, without losing sight of the complexity of the policy

process and the unique nature of environmental politics. Directly influenced by the politics of six governors, nearly two dozen federal
agencies, twelve U.S. senators, seventy-one U.S. representatives, hundreds of state legislators, and literally thousands of local officials,
Chesapeake Bay politics poses a particularly difficult conceptual
problem. (See figure 2.1 for a political map of the region.) It is the
politics of the nearly sixteen million individuals who live, work, and
play in the watershed, and the politics generated by the more than
three hundred environmental groups that focus on Bay-related issues,
as well as the politics of the thousands of businesses and industries
that employ Bay residents. What reducing this complex process to a
comprehensible level loses is hopefully offset by what is gained from
achieving a new level of conceptual order. In short, the risk of over-

Figure 2.1.   Political Map of Chesapeake Bay Watershed
Source: **Chesapeake Bay Program.**

simplification is outweighed by the danger of continuing in the absence of a conceptual framework. Only after a meaningful understanding of environmental politics is achieved can we appreciate the numerous challenges facing the environmental politics of the Chesapeake Bay and pursue a sensible political course for the Bay's environmental problems.

The explanation that follows attempts to create a conceptual model from the complex forces that drive the environmental politics of the Chesapeake Bay. It builds upon the logic and substance of several public policy theories (Downs 1972; Hofferbert 1974; Kiser and Ostrom 1982; Kingdon 1984; Moe 1984; Sabatier 1988, 1991; and Birkland 1997).[1] This study differs from many public policy works, however, in that it attempts to move beyond *describing* the stages of policy development and instead aims to explore the forces that drive and constrain public policy.[2] The theory is also distinct from much of the existing research in that it puts forth an "environmental policy theory," rather than applying a general public policy explanation to environmental politics.[3]

The explanation contends that, like the Bay itself, public policy tends to follow the course of least resistance, which all too often is not toward environmentally sound policy. While protecting the environment in the abstract has long been a popular theme among elected officials—at least as long as polls have shown broad public support for the environment—pursuing the long-term and often expensive environmental programs that are necessary to successfully restore ecosystems like the Chesapeake Bay has proved to be exceedingly difficult. The problem with enacting sound environmental public policy is not that it is unattainable from a technological or resource perspective; it is that the normal policy climate is generally hostile to the types of environmentally sound public policies that are necessary to restore a complex ecosystem like the Chesapeake Bay. The environmental policies that tend to emerge from this political climate tend to be reactionary, voluntary, and generally insufficient to meet the considerable challenges.

The dominant factors that comprise the policy context and that often constrain environmental policy outcomes are far from obvious. In the remainder of this chapter, four important political factors are explored and related to the politics of the Chesapeake Bay. In later chapters, these factors are further addressed by applying them to two of the Bay's specific environmental problems—nutrient management and crab restoration. The key political factors include these:

1. How economic primacy in the policy process creates a generally hostile climate for environmental politics
2. How America's fragmented political system fosters competitive forces that hamper environmental innovation and policy implementation at the state and local levels
3. How the dynamics of interest group formation and maintenance tend to favor industry and corporate groups over broad-based environmental groups
4. How events and leaders can coalesce to create limited windows of opportunity for environmental innovation

Though the political trends discussed here are not entirely novel, looking at them together and applying them to the Chesapeake Bay does reveal fresh insights into the challenges facing environmental restoration efforts. What is revealed is a fairly bleak political landscape that provides scant opportunities for successful passage of environmental legislation.[4] The forces that drive environmental degradation are deeply sown into the political soul of the United States, posing menacing challenges to those fighting to restore large ecosystems like the Chesapeake Bay.

The process serves as a poor reflection of the public's heightened interest and concern for environmental issues. In survey after survey, Americans have expressed their appreciation for the environment, with one recent survey showing that 71 percent of Americans believe that protecting the environment should be a high priority of the federal government.[5] Another recent survey found that Americans are generally willing to pay for a cleaner environment, with 68 percent of Americans agreeing that "we should protect the environment even if that might mean slower economic growth."[6] Likewise, 60 percent of Marylanders in a 2002 survey agreed that lawmakers should "work hard to protect the environment, even at the expense of new jobs."[7] The evidence that the general public is willing to absorb the cost of protecting public places goes beyond polling figures. Between 1998 and 2001, voters across the United States approved 529 local and state ballot measures, which allocated more than $19 billion to fund parks and public lands.[8] What we see later, however, is how the dynamics of the policy process often distort these strong and enduring public inputs to the point that public policies only vaguely reflect the public's environmental commitment.

"IT'S THE ECONOMY, STUPID": HOW ECONOMIC PRIMACY INFLUENCES ENVIRONMENTAL POLITICS

Politicians have long known what political scientists have more recently come to appreciate—economic concerns are a driving force behind American politics.[9] In a seminal study, Edward Tufte (1978) successfully made use of economic data to help explain American electoral outcomes. Since Tufte's work, the political science community has written a steady flow of essays and books on the subject (Kinder and Kiewiet 1979; Feldman 1982; Hibbs 1987; Erickson 1989; Lewis-Beck and Rice 1992; and Campbell and Garand 2000). Each of these works stresses economic conditions as a factor influencing American electoral politics. While political scientists debate the particulars of economic influences (i.e., whether the electorate responds to its perception of past, current, or future economic trends or whether voters respond to personal economic conditions or to the overall economic condition of the country), the fact that economic conditions influence electoral politics is no longer refuted.

The public policy implications for this tendency are as obvious as they are profound. The basic idea is that elected officials are either rewarded or punished at the polls depending on the public's perception of the economy. Knowing that voters respond to "pocketbook" issues, it is natural for political actors to stress public policies that support economic growth and prosperity.[10] Likewise, elected officials are particularly apprehensive to implement environmental policies that pose a direct threat to economic development. In short, policymakers are acutely aware of the political price of pursuing policies that challenge economic development, even if these policies promise to deliver a desired social or environmental good.[11]

The influence of economic considerations on environmental policy is clearly reflected in the increased acceptance of "cost-benefit" analysis for environmental regulations.[12] Early in President Ronald Reagan's first term, he signed executive order 12291, calling for extensive economic reviews of all major regulatory actions,[13] including environmental regulations.[14] While similar requirements have been supported by subsequent presidents and adopted in various states, many environmental advocates have argued that applying economic standards to environmental regulations stacks the deck against environmental policy.

It has been argued that the costs of regulations are often clear and well defined, with specific industries or the government having to pay a known amount, while the public benefits are broad and more abstract. The direct monetary impact is often compared to less quantifiable benefits, such as the value of increasing the amount of swimmable bodies of water, improving recreational fishing, or increasing the abundance of wildlife for observers and photographers. Moreover, the "nonuse" (or aesthetic) values of ecological resources and the potential health benefits for future generations derived from protecting the environment make estimating benefits even more difficult.[15]

Connelly and Smith (1999) make a distinction between three different "values" of the environment: instrumental, inherent, and intrinsic. The "instrumental value" of the environment is seen as its value as a human resource and is most often the only type of value considered in traditional cost-benefit analysis. The "inherent value" of nature, Connelly and Smith explain, is derived from the aesthetic or spiritual value people receive from experiencing nature, regardless of its economic promise. The third type of environmental value, hardly ever considered in cost-benefit analysis, is its "intrinsic value." The concept of "intrinsic value" suggests that the natural world has value independent from its material or aesthetic/spiritual utility to humans. For example, many environmental advocates would argue that vast areas of the Arctic National Wildlife Refuge (ANWR) should be preserved in its natural state even if doing so denies humans natural resources and even if few people will ever experience the majesty of the region.[16]

While the value of the environment can at times be abstract, the cost of policies is often clear and substantial.[17] The price is either paid directly by the public, as is the case with many environmental cleanup and restoration projects (like oyster restoration in the Bay or Superfund sights, more generally), or the price is supported by the particular producer of an environmental hazard, usually an industry through government regulations. It is estimated that in 1994, the EPA administered environmental programs with a total annual cost of approximately $140 billion,[18] 57 percent paid by private industry, 24 percent paid by local governments, 15 percent paid by federal government, and 4 percent paid by state governments (Vig and Kraft 1997, 24).[19]

Policies that call on the government to allocate funds directly from public sources are particularly contentious. Since government funds are limited and the activities government could pursue are unlimited, there exists a natural competition for public resources. Expensive environmental cleanup and restoration programs, like the Bay Program, invariably compete with other important government programs in areas such as education, public safety, and health care. Downturns in economic conditions only exasperate these competitive forces. Government officials are ultimately called on to either reduce spending in one area in order to increase environmental spending or to increase the available sources of public resources through higher taxes. In either case, the expense of environmental programs places fiscally-minded elected officials in a difficult position.

Regulatory measures that require industry to either clean up an environmental hazard it has already produced or to limit future production of environmental hazards carry their own economic costs and, consequently, political costs. Nearly without exception, such policies increase the production cost to industry. There are several ways that industries may deal with the cost of environmental regulations. The increased cost may either lead to lower earnings for the industry, lower salaries for the industry's employees, higher prices to the industry's consumers, or some combination of these outcomes. Since these off-putting economic outcomes are likely to carry negative political consequences, environmental regulation on industry becomes a difficult course of action.

The tension between environmentally sound and economically directed public policy has defined the course of environmental politics in the Chesapeake Bay area for over three decades. How to save the Bay's blue crabs without harming watermen? How to substantially reduce nutrient levels in the Bay without adversely affecting the agricultural industry? How to reduce the environmental impact of development without stifling growth and hurting real estate prices? How to improve sewage treatment plants without stressing local and state budgets? How to fund the roughly $20 billion that are estimated to be necessary for Bay restoration without derailing the region's economy?[20] In sum, how to restore the environmental health of the Bay while managing a regional economy that is larger and more dynamic than many European countries? All too often the "balance" between environmental concerns and economic interests is not a balance at all—economic factors take precedent.

DIVIDED GOVERNMENT AND THE RACE TO THE BOTTOM: HOW AMERICA'S FRAGMENTED POLITICAL SYSTEM WORKS AGAINST ENVIRONMENTAL INNOVATION

In 1968, Garrett Hardin first published his classic work "The Tragedy of the Commons," forever changing the way people view environmental problems. In this work, Hardin asks readers to imagine a pasture (i.e., a commons) that has been made available to a group of herdsmen and their cattle. Being rational beings, Hardin argues, each herdsman would try to keep as many cattle on the commons as possible, since each herdsman seeks to maximize his individual gain. Hardin suggests that each herdsman grapples with the following question, "What is the utility of adding one more cow to my herd?" For each herdsman, there is both a positive and a negative to increasing the herd. The positive is that the individual herdsman would gain the proceeds from another animal, a benefit that the herdsman would not have to share. The negative is that another cow would contribute to the overgrazing of the commons, a negative effect that would be shared by each herdsman. Since the individual herdsman receives all the positive, but shares the negative effects of adding additional cows, the incentive is to keep adding more and more cows to the commons. The long-term consequence is that the short-term thinking of individual herdsman eventually destroys the common area.[21]

While a fascinating theory that helps to explain why industries left to their own accord would be unlikely to sustain healthy environmental conditions, Hardin's lessons have other, less explored, political implications. Local and state governments in this country act very much like the herdsmen that Hardin described. Instead of desiring additional cows, these subnational governments consider the addition of industry or development to their jurisdiction. They grapple with a similar version of the herdsman's question, "What is the utility of adding one more industry or development project to this area?" Since the positive political impact of industry and development (i.e., well-paying jobs and additional tax revenue) tends to be localized and the environmental conse-

quences of industry are likely to extend well beyond political boundaries, Hardin's logic holds. Local and state governments acting as rational actors see it as sensible to add more and more industry and development to their jurisdictions.

The main difference between Hardin's cattle metaphor and the
forces at play in subnational politics is that local and state governments
cannot simply add new industries to their jurisdictions the way that
Hardin's herdsmen add cattle. These governmental units compete to attract new industry and development to their areas and seek to retain existing sources of revenue.[22] The end result is what one political analyst
described as a "race to the bottom" in which subnational governments
are drawn into a competitive race to make their jurisdictions as attractive to industry and development as possible.[23] Because of the economic
consequences of many environmental policies, one manner in which
subnational governments can make an area attractive to industry is by
minimizing the impact of environmental regulations. At the very least,
the competitive race to attract industry can stifle environmental innovation at the local and state levels. Moreover, competition may also create
a situation in which federally mandated regulations are met with resistance at the state and local levels.[24]

Given this dynamic, it is not surprising that a recent study of environmental management at the state level conducted by Professor Barry
Rabe (1997) of the University of Michigan's School of Public Health
found that "there is growing reason to worry about how effectively
states generally handle core functions either delegated to them under
federal programs or left exclusively to their oversight" (41). Rabe finds
that states have employed highly variable water quality, air quality, and
waste management standards, making enforcement of federal air and
water standards difficult or impossible in many states. Rabe points to
the states of Alabama and Texas as prime examples of the state trend to
resist environmental controls. While these states have extensive estuaries and beaches and both states consistently report that their beaches
and estuaries meet the swimmability goals of the Clean Water Act, neither state conducts regular monitoring of its marine areas, making such
claims problematic.

The consequences of these competitive forces can have a tremendous impact on the environmental politics of the Chesapeake Bay.
Throughout the Bay area there are some 1,650 local governments and
four major metropolitan areas (i.e., Baltimore, Norfolk, Richmond, and

Washington), each with a desire to promote economic development and prosperity. Moreover, many of the jurisdictions that have the greatest impact on water quality, areas with intense farming and animal production activities, such as Lancaster, Pennsylvania, are located a considerable distance from the Bay. Likewise, there are six states in the Bay watershed, three of which are upstream states, meaning that they do not have a single acre of Bay shoreline to protect. The most important upstream state is Pennsylvania, which comprises a larger percent of the Chesapeake Bay drainage basin than any other state (35 percent).[25] It is difficult to imagine these areas actively and voluntarily pursuing costly land management practices to protect a distant ecosystem.

Nevertheless, reliance on voluntary action by local government and industry has historically been the dominant approach taken by the Chesapeake Bay restoration effort. Favero (1997) describes the voluntary approach as one that stresses education and moral suasion, rather than regulation. It is based on the assumption that local governments and the industries that fall under local control will voluntarily adopt environmentally sound methods once they become aware of the harmful effects of their current methods. It is grounded in the somewhat naive belief that education can outweigh economic pressures and competitive forces, making coercive actions by government unnecessary.

FREE RIDING: UNDERSTANDING THE INTEREST GROUP IMBALANCE IN ENVIRONMENTAL POLITICS

Given the influence of economic concerns over U.S. public policy and that industry interests have vast resources at their disposal to influence the political process, it should not be surprising that the political influence of industry often outweighs the competing voice of environmental groups. Many political scientists and economists have come to believe that the interest group imbalance runs even deeper than is commonly thought. Many of these thinkers build on the ideas presented in a classic work published by Mancur Olson in 1965, *The Logic of Collective Action.*

Olson's interest group theory is most easily comprehended by utilizing a simple thought experiment. Imagine for a moment a large dormitory of over a thousand residents in which each resident occupies a private room. In this dormitory, each person controls her own thermostat and is individually responsible for paying her heating and cooling bills. Now, imagine that the walls of the dorm rooms are such that they extend to just below the ceiling, allowing air to freely flow from one room to the next. Olson's theory suggests that in a situation like this, each resident in the dorm would have an incentive to turn her heat down to just below the temperature of her neighbor's room, or in the summer to raise her thermostat to just above her neighbors'. In doing so, the individual would enjoy the benefits of the group (i.e., warm air in the winter and cool air in the summer) without having to bear the individual expense of paying large heating and cooling costs. This phenomenon is commonly referred to as the free-rider problem—the problem of individuals enjoying the benefits of groups without contributing to the groups.

Olson applies this problem to the issue of interest group formation and concludes that large groups that seek broad benefits, such as citizen-based environmental groups, are likely to have less of an impact on the political system than business groups. He argues that since individuals enjoy the public benefits these groups seek (e.g., clean air and water) whether or not they contribute to the group, there is a strong incentive for potential members to free ride. This problem is particularly acute for large groups, since it is hard for individuals to see the direct result of their individual contribution to the group, and, likewise, it is difficult for a large group to notice whether a single potential member fails to contribute. These problems combine to work against the formation and maintenance of citizen-based interest groups working to restore the Bay.

Olson argues that several factors make the problem of free riding less acute for industry or business groups. First, industry groups tend to seek "selective benefits" (i.e., benefits that only the particular industry will enjoy), such as lower industry-specific taxes or the elimination of a particular regulation. Since the aim is focused on specific material rewards, not more abstract benefits that are enjoyed by the entire community, the incentive to participate is increased. Also, since individual industries comprise a relatively small number of like-minded members, the size factor is less of a burden for these groups than it is for citizen groups, further reducing the tendency to free ride. Each group member (a business or producer of some good or service) is aware of the direct impact that its contribution has on the group that represents the industry. Likewise, the group can easily monitor the participation of the individual members, since there are relatively few members.

The net result, according to Olson, is that the interests of industry and business are much more likely to be meaningfully represented in interest group politics than the broad-based interests of groups that fight for things like environmental protection. Olson (1965) writes, "There is a systematic tendency for 'exploitation' of the great by the small" (29). In short, the fear is that the organization and maintenance difficulties faced by broad-based groups, such as environmental groups, lead to unequal political resources (i.e., money, time, and expertise), which in turn leads to an unequal political voice for these groups.[26] Moreover, Baumgartner and Jones (1993) suggest the interest imbalance is particularly prevalent at the local level since "local business elites are better able to affect political outcomes in small governments, because their resources are critical to the causes of local politicians" (222).

At the national level, the imbalance between groups fighting to protect the environment and those representing industry and corporate America has been well documented.[27] Discussing this issue, Christopher Bosso (1997) writes that the reality is that environmental groups "are seriously outgunned by the battalions of corporate lobbyists, the resources industries pour into their lobbying efforts, and, more bluntly, by the millions of dollars in campaign contributions that flow into Congress from corporate political action committees." Bosso argues that despite the considerable amount that environmental groups spend attempting to influence public policy, in comparison to the vast resources of industry and corporate America, the nation's environmental lobby amounts to little more than a political "bauble" (65).

This interest group imbalance is also evident in the politics of the Chesapeake Bay. The Chesapeake Bay Foundation (CBF) is the largest and most active public interest environmental group representing the Chesapeake Bay.[28] CBF began its environmental activities in 1967, the year the organization printed its first "Save the Bay" bumper sticker.[29] Over the years, support for the organization has substantially increased, making it one of the most successful regional environmental groups in the nation. In the year 2000 alone, CBF raised over $24 million in revenue and had expenditures totaling more than $13 million.[30] Currently, the group operates nine offices in four states—Maryland, Virginia, Pennsylvania, and Delaware—and enjoys the support of approximately a hundred thousand dues-paying members. Its primary activities include conducting educational programs throughout the watershed, promoting public policy, and monitoring the implementation of the Bay restoration programs.

While the Chesapeake Bay Foundation represents an interest group success story, seemingly defying Olson's expectations for such citizen-based groups, as a *political* organization it is far less impressive than its industry competitors. CBF does not employ a single full-time lobbyist, has no affiliated political action committee, has never contributed any money to political campaigns, and has no organized legal defense fund.[31] Since CBF has no full-time lobbyist, relying instead on the executive directors and staff attorneys in its state offices to conduct most of the group's lobbying, it is difficult to estimate exactly how much time and energy CBF spends advocating public policy at the state and federal levels. Mike Shultz, vice president of public affairs at CBF, estimates the organization employs the equivalent of one half-time employee for these activities. Mike Hirshfield, the head of CBF's advocacy programs from 1996 through 2001,[32] estimates the amount of lobbying at CBF to be somewhat higher, with the organization employing the equivalent of about three full-time lobbyists.[33] In any case, it is difficult to imagine the group having much of a sustained political impact given the fact that Bay-related issues involve the legislative and executive bodies of six states and the federal government.

Data from the National Institute on Money in State Politics (2002), which tracks political contributions made to candidates running for state office, offers valuable insights into the comparative political strength of groups like CBF to their industry counterparts. This data reveals that political contributors gave over $34 million in Maryland (1998) and $21 million in Virginia (1999).[34] In both states, industries that are most directly affected by environmental regulations are active political contributors—for example, real estate, $1,591,580 (Maryland) and $672,246 (Virginia); construction, $1,586,219 (Maryland) and $815,166 (Virginia); transportation, $623,176 (Maryland) and $353,367 (Virginia); agriculture, $448,609 (Maryland) and $74,894 (Virginia); and oil/gas, $224,676 (Maryland) and $102,189 (Virginia). In comparison, pro-environment/conservation groups gave merely $5,396 in Maryland and recorded no political contributions in Virginia during these recent political cycles. Considering that most of the industry groups mentioned previously maintain full-time lobbying operations, something environmental groups in the area lack, the comparative political strength of industry is impressive.

THE POLICY CYCLE, FOCUSING EVENTS, AND POLITICAL LEADERS: MAKING THE MOST OF LIMITED OPPORTUNITIES FOR ENVIRONMENTAL INNOVATION

Thus far, we have seen how economic primacy, America's divided political structure, and interest group politics present substantial challenges for environmentally friendly public policy. However, the fact remains that substantive environmental public policy does periodically work its way through the political system. At the national level, the Clean Air Act of 1970 and the Clean Water Act of 1972 provide clear examples of public policy that was enacted despite the objection of both industry and powerful political foes. At the state level, Maryland's 1984 Critical Areas Act, its rockfish moratorium, its phosphate detergent ban, and, more recently, its 1998 Water Improvement Act (discussed later) serve as similar examples. Given the substantial obstacles discussed previously, it is important to understand how these and other environmental innovations have been successfully achieved.

To address this issue, it is useful to consider Anthony Downs's 1972 essay, "Up and Down with Ecology."[35] In this essay, Downs argues that public policy goes through an "issue-attention" cycle, in which "problems suddenly leap into prominence, remain there for a short time, and then—though still largely unresolved—gradually fade from the center of public attention."[36] The cycle, according to Downs, has five stages:

1. *The pre-problem stage.* In this stage an undesirable condition, such as environmental degradation, exists but it has yet to capture a substantial amount of public attention.
2. *The alarmed discovery and euphoric enthusiasm stage.* As a result of some dramatic occurrence, such as the outbreak of a pollutant-related health problem, the public becomes aware of a problem and is enthusiastic about society's ability to solve the problem.
3. *The cost realization stage.* In this stage, the public comes to realize that the cost of solving the problem is relatively high and may result in sacrifices by large segments of the society or the society as a whole.
4. *The decline of intense public interest stage.* Upon realizing the cost and difficulty of addressing the issue, the general public's attention gradually moves away from the issue.

5. *The post-problem stage.* In this stage, public attention moves "into a prolonged limbo—a twilight realm of lesser attention or spasmodic recurrences of interests."[37]

It is apparent that environmental politics in this country has passed through the first four stages that Downs describes and is currently in the "post-problem stage." During the pre-problem stage, prior to the 1960s, environmental problems received relatively little public attention, and the modern environmental movement, with its emphasis on politics, had yet to materialize. By the late 1960s and early 1970s, environmental concerns had entered the alarmed discovery and euphoric enthusiasm stage. This short-lived period of heightened public concern and boundless optimism was followed by the cost realization stage in the late 1970s. As Downs suggests, this stage was followed by the current period, the post-problem stage, a period in which environmental problems have not disappeared, but acute attention and optimism have subsided.

Downs's model suggests that the biggest opportunity for enacting meaningful environmental public policy has come and gone—that is, the alarmed discovery and euphoric enthusiasm stage. This is not to say that the current post-problem stage of environmental politics is without its opportunities. Several studies (Truman 1951; Cobb and Elder 1983; Kingdon 1984; and Birkland 1997) help to explain how windows of opportunity periodically open as a response to particular threats or disturbances.[38] These focusing events provide policy entrepreneurs (i.e., advocates for policy change) brief opportunities to form winning coalitions and to enact meaningful policy innovations. Downs (1972) describes these opportunities in this way:

> The greater the apparent threat from visible forms of pollution and the more vividly this can be dramatized, the more public support environmental improvement will receive and the longer it will sustain public interest. Ironically, the cause of ecologists would therefore benefit from an environmental disaster like "killer smog" that would choke thousands to death in a few days. (46–47)

While environmental policy entrepreneurs work year in and year out to pass environmental legislation, their efforts during normal conditions are rarely sufficient to overcome the considerable obstacles to environmental policy. In the wake of a focusing event, however, proposals that failed in previous years may gain sufficient support to win approval. Under these conditions, champions of environmental policy are able to take advantage of a brief period of public scrutiny to form a winning legislative coalition. But as time passes and public attention fades, the ephemeral opportunity comes to an end. These brief periods of opportunity aside, Downs and others contend that the "normal" policy context, the post-problem stage, is poorly suited for enacting environmental legislation. Building on this logic, it is easy to see how the post-problem setting may actually evolve into something more harmful than merely a period of policy stagnation; it is not difficult to comprehend the post-problem stage as a period in which hard-fought environmental gains are incrementally eroded away. Since the industry forces that feel the brunt of most environmental regulations do not rely on a sustained public outcry to fuel their political efforts, as environmental groups do, it is likely that industry forces are able to maintain more consistent political pressure than their environmental counterparts. If this is the case, it is likely that industry interests will be most successful in overturning environmental gains when public interest is relatively low, making the post-problem stage a fertile setting for their efforts.

The post-problem struggle to maintain environmental policy at the national level can be seen in several legislative measures proposed to "reform" the EPA during the 1990s. With environmental attention waning and following the 1994 takeover of Congress by the Republican Party, Congress proposed several reform measures in the mid-1990s. These reforms included cutting EPA funding by more than 20 percent, requiring all regulations to undergo a cost-benefit analysis, and giving states far greater authority to interpret and enforce federal environmental regulations.[39]

The politics of the Chesapeake Bay also provides evidence for the policy cycle. The early period of excitement about the Bay restoration effort, at its height during the mid-1980s, has come and gone. This was a period when Marylanders enthusiastically shouted "Save the Bay" and other words of encouragement as Maryland's environmental Governor Harry Hughes traveled across the state spreading his environmental message. It was a time of optimism, when hard-hitting legislation was enacted such as land use restrictions, a moratorium on rockfish, and a phosphate detergent ban. During the early 1980s, the prospect of a clean Bay that promised countless recreational activities and supported a vibrant fishing industry seemed within grasp. Unfortunately, this stage, what Downs would refer to as the alarmed discovery and euphoric enthusiasm stage, had passed by the late 1980s, as Bay politics passed into the more contentious and politically problematic stages of public policy.

As public policy research suggests, the post-problem period is not without its opportunities for environmental progress. An example of this type of window of opportunity occurred in the summer of 1997. Several areas of the Chesapeake Bay experienced outbreaks of *Pfiesteria*, a toxic microorganism. The EPA believes that *Pfiesteria* was the primary cause of a 1997 fish kill that led to the death of an estimated fifty thousand Bay fish. Beyond the threat to wildlife, the EPA cites 1997 medical evidence that "strongly suggested that exposure to an active outbreak of *Pfiesteria* may result in significant, but probably temporary, health impacts on humans."[40] Outbreaks of the microorganism are known to be associated with nutrient overenrichment, a phenomenon that has been linked to farm runoff and other sources of nutrient loading to the Bay (see chapter 3 for a detailed discussion of the impact of nutrient overloading).

The health hazard and intense media attention that followed the outbreak created a prime condition for legislative action. In 1998, the U.S. Congress allocated a total of $18 million to *Pfiesteria*-related programs and research. This amount nearly equaled the amount the EPA was allocated to fund all Chesapeake Bay Programs in 1998. Maryland's state government also took decisive action following the *Pfiesteria* outbreak. In the final hours of the 1998 General Assembly session, state legislators approved the 1998 Water Quality Improvement Act. Overcoming intense pressure from Maryland's farm industry, the act set requirements for Maryland farmers to complete and implement *mandatory* nutrient management plans by set dates. Though the farming community continues to resist mandatory regulations and the majority of farmers have not met the schedule, the controversial legislation was a move away from the voluntary incentive-based approach of the past and is viewed as a major step in the Bay restoration effort.

PUTTING THE PIECES TOGETHER

Several factors combine to foster a political climate that is ill suited for sustaining long-term environmentally sound public policy. While brief

47

periods of opportunity may arise from time to time, the normal political setting creates tremendous obstacles for environmental public policy. It is not surprising that the National Commission on the Environment, an environmental panel including four former administrators of the EPA, commented in a 1993 report, "The U.S. statutory and regulatory system is woefully inadequate, cumbersome, and sometimes even perverse in respect to environmental issues"[41] and that a more recent assessment of environmental regulatory policy in the United States by Davies and Mazurek (1997) concluded, "The pollution control regulatory system is deeply and fundamentally flawed" (2).[42]

Figure 2.2 graphically illustrates the conceptual framework outlined in this chapter. The figure shows how the public concern that goes into the policy process is constrained by powerful factors that are built into the political system (i.e., economic primacy in the policy process, competition among local and state governments, and interest group imbalance). At the end of the funnel, environmental champions work the "policy pump," trying to successfully produce sound environmental policies. But in the absence of a focusing event, it is rare that sufficient pressure builds within the system to allow meaningful environmental solutions to emerge. The policies that trickle out of the funnel are generally inadequate to address the Bay's considerable problems and serve as a poor reflection of the public's desire for meaningful environmental

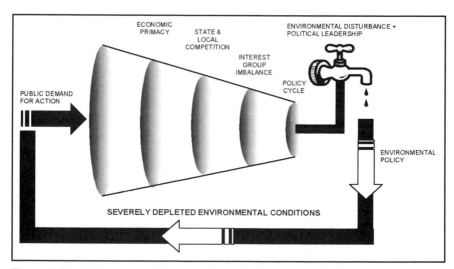

Figure 2.2.   A Conceptual Framework for Environmental Policy
Graphic Design by Christine Jamison.

progress. This process unfolds despite widespread public support for environmental policies, the existence of available technologies and scientific support, and the sincere concern and hard work of many policymakers and community leaders.

The inability of the political process to adequately address environmental problems does not imply that the political context will lead to a wholesale neglect of environmental issues. So long as the electorate continues to register environmental issues as important public policy concerns, these issues will retain a place in the policy process.[43] The political course of least resistance leads political actors to engage environmental problems, at least up to the point in which environmental policies threaten economic development or demand substantial public resources. The greatest danger from the political process is not that it will ignore environmental issues; it is that the inadequate and reactionary environmental policies that tend to emerge become acceptable substitutes for meaningful environmental planning and long-term solutions.

The Bay's greatest danger is the emergence of a cozy political partnership that provides plenty of opportunities for "success," but that produces few tangible environmental accomplishments. In such a situation, well-intentioned policymakers take credit for producing a steady flow of agreements, reports, and voluntary programs. Funding for environmental programs incrementally increases with each passing year. The scientific community is kept active researching and monitoring the health of the ecosystem. Collaborative programs provide countless opportunities for environmental groups and industry representatives to participate in the ongoing public policy debate.[44] And occasionally, even hard-hitting regulatory actions make their way through the system. Collectively, the restoration effort is billed as the nation's premier watershed restoration program and is promoted as a model for estuarine restoration programs worldwide. All the while, decades pass and the Bay's most basic environmental indicators suggest little if any sustained improvement.

Part II

NUTRIENT MANAGEMENT AND BAY POLITICS

3

Swimming against the Tide

Nutrient Reduction Efforts in the Bay Watershed

In 2001, water quality monitoring data from the Bay's largest tributaries revealed no discernable trends in nutrient loads, despite modeling results showing a 15 percent reduction in the amount of nitrogen entering the Chesapeake Bay from 1985–2000.

> —Chesapeake Bay Commission (2001b), *Seeking Solutions: Chesapeake Bay Commission, Annual Report*

If they had a storm like Tropical Storm Agnes 600 years ago, it would not have made a whole lot of difference. This area was all woodland and filtered.

> —Harry Hughes (2002), governor of Maryland 1979–1987

The introduction of nutrients into the Chesapeake Bay is a natural and necessary function of this ecosystem. Prior to human development, nutrients entered the Bay from its rivers, tributaries, and shoreline as the natural by-product of nutrient-rich runoff from forested lands. In this natural condition, a steady supply of nutrients entered the Bay, feeding a healthy population of phytoplankton (tiny aquatic vegetation) and nourishing massive expanses of underwater grasses. The watershed's high land-to-water ratio provided the Bay with a plentiful supply of nutrients and helped to make the Chesapeake Bay one of the most productive ecosystems on earth. Toward the bottom of the food chain, small fish and other animals fed on the aquatic vegetation and in turn provided food for larger predators. Waste produced by the Bay's aquatic animals reintroduced nutrients into the Bay, allowing the Bay's nutrient loads to be used and reused in an efficient manner. In time, nutrients that entered the Bay from its shores and tributaries were flushed out of the system by outgoing tides, only to be replaced by fresh loads of nutrients—completing the natural cycle and maintaining a healthy balance.[1]

In its natural state, the system worked remarkably well. The Bay used the available nutrients efficiently, supplying an essential resource to the food chain. With human development, however, the natural process of nutrient enrichment has been severely altered. The scientific term for an increased rate of organic matter supplied to an ecosystem is *eutrophication*.[2] Today, nutrients (most importantly, phosphorus and nitrogen) enter the Bay in massive quantities as the by-products of agricultural production (i.e., fertilizers and animal waste), sewage plants, storm-water runoff, septic tanks, and combustion engines.[3] Recent studies estimate that around 287 million pounds of nitrogen and 20 million pounds of phosphorus are introduced to the Bay each year, the vast majority of which is the direct result of human activity.[4] It has been estimated that nutrient levels are currently seven times higher than they were prior to human development.[5]

There are three general classifications of nutrients—point source nutrients, nonpoint source nutrients, and atmospheric nutrients. Point source nutrients enter the Bay through a specific identifiable location, such as a pipe leaving a sewage treatment facility.[6] Roughly a quarter of the Bay's nutrients enter the Bay from point sources; most of these nutrients enter from the nearly 300 major sewage treatment plants in the watershed. Nonpoint source nutrients enter the Bay from all other ground sources, including agricultural runoff and septic tank seepage. Over half of the human-produced nitrogen and phosphorus entering the Bay arrives from nonpoint sources, with agricultural runoff being the chief culprit (see figures 3.1 and 3.2). The remaining nutrients enter the Bay as atmospheric fallout (i.e., air pollution) caused by the region's ever-growing number of cars, lawn mowers, boats, and power plants.

These externalities (i.e., unwanted by-products of human activity) overfertilize the Bay's phytoplankton, causing massive algae blooms in the spring and summer. The algae blooms cloud the water, depriving aquatic grasses and other living resources of life-supporting sunlight. Moreover, when the phytoplankton dies, it falls to the bottom of the Bay and decomposes, a process that consumes considerable amounts of

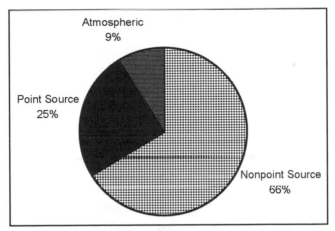

Figure 3.1. Sources of Phosphorus Pollution to the Bay, 1996. *Source:* **Chesapeake Bay Program (1999c, 24).**

dissolved oxygen, further reducing the life-supporting ability of the Bay. In scientific terms, extreme cases of oxygen depletion are referred to as *anoxia* (i.e., the nearly complete depletion of dissolved oxygen in water) and *hypoxia* (dissolved oxygen concentrations lower than required by indigenous organisms).[7] Horton and Eichbaum (1991, 18) explain the environmental consequences of anoxia: "The bottom line is that massive regions of the Bay may become as devoid of oxygen as the surface of the moon. Large portions of the Bay, which still look clean and vital

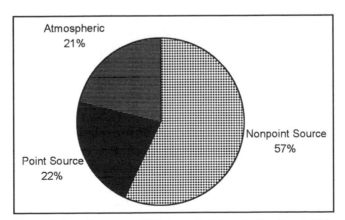

Figure 3.2. Sources of Nitrogen Pollution to the Bay, 1996. *Source:* **Chesapeake Bay Program (1999c, 24).**

to the eye of a boater sailing across them, may in fact be as hostile to fish and crabs as a sandy desert." The long-term consequence and the ultimate irony of the situation is that overfertilization depletes the Bay of its ability to support life, leaving much of the Bay a barren wasteland (see figure 3.3 for the oxygen requirements for several Bay species).[8]

Not only can oxygen depletion leave large areas of the Bay lifeless, but rapid declines in oxygen levels can also lead to massive fish kills in once vibrant areas. While it is difficult to estimate how much aquatic life has been lost to oxygen depletion in recent years, the Maryland Department of the Environment estimates that over 200,000 fish were lost to oxygen depletion in 1999 alone. In the summer of 2001, floating dead fish, the telltale sign of an oxygen-related fish kill, were widely reported in the areas of the Bay including Herring Bay, Magothy River, and the Severn River. While oxygen-related fish kills have occurred in the Bay for many years, Harley Speir, head of the biological monitoring and analysis program for the Maryland Department of Natural Resources Fisheries Service, believes, "This [low oxygen levels] is not getting any better, and we're going to have to struggle with the problem."

Beyond the harmful effects of oxygen depletion and reduced sunlight, scientists have linked nutrient loading to toxic algae blooms that also threaten the Bay's aquatic resources.[9] Scientists have identified nutrient-saturated water as a prime factor promoting toxic algae blooms. The Bay's most widely reported toxic bloom occurred in 1997. That year, *Pfiesteria,* a toxic microorganism, led to the death of tens of thousands of fish in the Bay. Since 1997, increased monitoring has revealed a regular occurrence of *Pfiesteria* and other dangerous algae forms in the Bay, though the widespread fish kills reported in 1997 have not reoccurred.[10] More recently, a strain of the "mahogany tide," a form of algae common in the Bay, was found to be capable of producing a toxin that can contaminate shellfish. Moreover, unknown varieties of algae, with unknown environmental and health consequences, have also been found in recent studies.[11]

Toxic algae has also been linked to human illness. A 1998 study (Grattan et al.) found significant cognitive deficits (i.e., memory loss and difficulty learning) in humans who were exposed to *Pfiesteria.* The issue began to attract attention during the summer of 1997 when Dr. Ritchie Shoemaker, a physician practicing on the Eastern Shore of Maryland, began treating patients for symptoms attributed to *Pfiesteria* exposure. The symptoms included headaches, flu-like muscle aches, trouble with

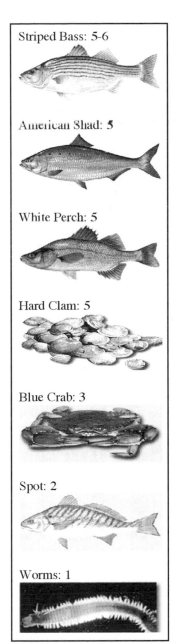

Striped Bass: 5-6

American Shad: 5

White Perch: 5

Hard Clam: 5

Blue Crab: 3

Spot: 2

Worms: 1

Figure 3.3.   Dissolved Oxygen Criteria: Milligrams of Oxygen per Liter of Water *Source:* **Blankenship (2001a).**

memory, and dime-sized lesions on patients' lower extremities.[12] While the impact of *Pfiesteria* on humans is now believed to be temporary, the long-term impact of *Pfiesteria* toxins on the human brain is simply unknown. Another algae, *Chattonella verruculosa*, which produces the same toxin that has sickened people in the Gulf of Mexico, has also been found in low levels in Maryland waters. Moreover, blue-green algae, a species that can kill domestic animals if consumed, bloomed in 2001 on the Potomac and Sassafras Rivers. As recently as the winter of 2002, an oyster ban was placed on large portions of the Potomac after a toxic algae (*Dinophysis acuminata*) was found to have contaminated shellfish in that area. The prevalence and increased awareness of these toxic algae blooms has made nutrient reduction not only an environmental concern, but also a persistent public safety issue for residents of the Bay area and consumers of Chesapeake Bay shellfish.

THE DIFFICULTY OF ACHIEVING NUTRIENT REDUCTIONS

The deleterious consequences of nutrient loading have long been recognized as the single greatest threat to the long-term health of the Chesapeake Bay. As early as 1972, when Tropical Storm Agnes inundated the Bay with massive nutrient loads, the scientific community began to vocalize its concern regarding the long-term dangers of nutrient loading. Some have argued that this event led to a paradigm shift within the scientific community and later the general public—causing people to abandon the prevailing view of the Bay as an extension of the sea and instead to see the Bay as a distinct ecosystem that is dominated by the influences of its watershed.[13] Given that the land-to-water ratio for the Chesapeake Bay is larger than any other body of water on the planet, it is not surprising that land use practices throughout the watershed greatly influence water quality in the Bay.[14]

The EPA's early assessment of the Bay, completed in the early 1980s, confirmed the growing concern among scientists that the Bay was being severely altered by nutrient loading. Moreover, from its inception in 1983, the Chesapeake Bay Program acknowledged nutrient loading as the Bay's primary health problem and has made reducing this environmental threat its chief restoration objective for nearly two decades.[15] The aim of reducing nutrient pollutants was the driving force behind the Second Bay Agreement (1987) and has helped to focus the restoration effort throughout the 1990s. In the Second Bay Agreement, the Chesapeake Bay Program and its restoration partners set the ambitious goal of reducing the level of controllable nutrients entering the Bay by 40 percent of the 1985 levels by the year 2000 (discussed in detail later).

The Chesapeake Bay Program has pursued a multipronged management strategy that reflects the multiple sources of nutrients entering the Bay. The appendix outlines the major events and programs that have influenced nutrient management in the Bay watershed in recent years, as well as several of the factors that have worked against the nutrient reduction effort. The table is divided into two columns: the column on the left lists major initiatives implemented with nutrient reduction as a primary goal, and the column on the right lists the circumstances that have complicated the task of nutrient reduction. The table reveals the complexity and difficulty of meaningfully addressing this long-term environmental problem.

The most obvious factor working against nutrient reduction efforts is that the number of people residing in the Bay watershed has steadily grown over the last century and is likely to substantially increase in future years. Conservative estimates predict the population in the area will reach eighteen million by 2020, a doubling in the area's population since the early 1950s.[16] Moreover, the amount of energy individuals consume in their homes, the number of cars they operate, the number of miles they drive, and the amount of land that is developed for residential and consumer use have each increased at even higher rates than population growth. Add to this the intensification of farming practices, increased sewage loads, and aging storm water systems, and the difficulty of nutrient management starts to come into focus.

Each of these factors complicates nutrient management efforts. For example, it is estimated that each new resident of the watershed adds to the area 1,300 pounds of solid waste per year, which, depending on how it is treated, may substantially affect nutrient loads entering the Bay.[17] Currently, 1.5 billion gallons of treated sewage flows into the Bay each day.[18] More vehicles on the road and increased production by utility companies lead to additional nitrogen oxide in the atmosphere and, consequently, more nitrogen entering the Bay. The development of the land removes natural buffers and allows nutrient-rich runoff to enter the Bay through storm water systems more quickly and in higher concentrations than would occur from undeveloped land. The intensification of farm practices leads to the production of massive amounts of animal waste, mostly from poultry, dairy, and hog farms, as well as nutrient loading from fertilizers. These agricultural by-products, much of which come from states that do not border the Bay, enter as runoff and substantially impact nutrient levels.

While the pressures of population growth and development complicate the matter, they do not pose insurmountable obstacles for effective nutrient management. Several technological advances and general improvements in our scientific understanding of nutrient loading have led to promising innovations that may reduce nutrient loading. Some of these innovations include the following:

1. *Phosphate-free detergents.* The ability to produce detergents that are effective, yet free of phosphates, has allowed lawmakers in Virginia, Pennsylvania, and Maryland to ban the substance in detergents. More than any other development, the phosphate ban is credited with reducing the amount of phosphorus entering the Bay.[19]

2. *Biological nutrient removal (BNR) systems.* Biological nutrient removal systems enable sewage treatment plants to eliminate a substantial portion of the waterborne nutrients that they discharge into the Bay, lowering the nitrogen effluence from 18 milligrams per liter to as low as 3 milligrams per liter.[20]

3. *Efficient septic systems.* A quarter of the households in the watershed, many of them in rural areas near the Bay's tributaries and shores, depend on septic systems for sewage treatment. It is estimated that 33 million pounds of nitrogen enter the Bay each year as a result of loading from septic systems.[21] Modern improvements in septic system technology enable nutrient loads from this source to be substantially reduced.

4. *Emission control technologies.* Advances in emission control technologies are capable of reducing airborne pollutants that enter the Bay from nitrogen oxide, a by-product of combustion engines. Though resisted by automobile producers and utility providers, amendments to the Clean Air Act in 1990 may help to offset the impact of the growing number of vehicles and utility plants in the region.

5. *Animal feed additives.* Successful experiments with feed additives, such as phytase, an enzyme that substantially improves the

digestion of phosphorus in poultry and swine, are opening new doors in the struggle to reduce nutrient waste. With animals making better use of phosphorus in feed, the need to supplement feed with phosphorus is reduced and the level of phosphorus in animal manure also drops. Tests on poultry have found as much as a 33 percent reduction in the phosphorus level of chicken manure when poultry are fed phytase additives.

6. *Agricultural best management practices (BMPs).*[22] BMPs are designed to reduce the harmful impact of agriculture by minimizing the amount of nutrient runoff produced through agricultural practices (discussed in detail in chapter 4). BMP techniques include limiting fertilizer use to only what is necessary for healthy crops, creating vegetation and forest buffers, practicing conservation tillage, and installing manure storage structures and manure runoff controls.

7. *Smart growth.*[23] While "smart growth" practices have become synonymous with the antisprawl movement of the last decade, the practices encompass far more than merely limiting urban sprawl. Many smart growth initiatives limit the amount of pollutants entering the Bay (mostly nitrogen oxide from automobile engines) and maximize the innate filtering process of natural lands. Smart growth initiatives include preserving natural areas around the Bay, promoting housing projects near urban centers, improving mass transit, clustering homes to preserve open spaces, and restoring existing developed lands.

Though technological innovations and scientific knowledge provide useful mechanisms for reducing the harmful impact of nutrients, these developments are rarely utilized to their full potential. Quite simply, the price to government and the private sector of implementing nutrient-sensitive technologies and practices has tended to impede nutrient reduction efforts. For example, the Maryland Department of Natural Resources recently estimated that the cost of achieving Maryland's stated nutrient and sediment goals for the Chesapeake Bay would exceed $6.8 billion over a seven-year period. The Maryland report projects a $4.4 billion difference between required funding and current funding sources.[24]

To date, efforts by the EPA's Chesapeake Bay Program and other organizations working to reduce the amount of nutrients entering the

Bay have led to mixed results. The attempt to limit nutrient loading from point sources has been moderately successful. Nutrient reductions in these areas have primarily resulted from the Bay states adopting phosphate detergent bans between 1985 and 1990. By removing phosphorus from detergents, lawmakers were able to substantially reduce the amount of phosphorus entering wastewater treatment plants and, consequently, reduce the amount of phosphorus flowing from these plants into the Bay. Additional gains have resulted from some sewage treatment plants, 65 out of the 288 major treatment plants, implementing biological nutrient removal (BNR) technologies. Unlike previous sewage treatment practices that concentrated primarily on removing organic content from wastewater, BNR technologies enable sewage treatment plants to reduce nutrients, in addition to organic matter.

While BNR technologies hold a great deal of promise for the Bay, reducing nitrogen effluence from roughly 18 milligrams per liter to as low as 3 milligrams per liter, the cost of these upgrades has made sewage treatment facilities slow to adopt biological nutrient removal systems. Among the sewage treatment facilities that implemented BNR technologies in the region, not one facility implements the most advanced technologies that reduce nitrogen effluence to the lowest possible level—that is, 3 milligrams per liter. Typical BNR systems in the Bay result in nitrogen effluence levels of about 6 milligrams per liter, twice as high as what the best technology can provide.[25] The Bay states have derived even fewer results from advances in septic system technology, which can also substantially reduce the amount of nutrients that enter the Bay as a consequence of human waste. The increased cost of efficient septic systems and the fact that not one of the Bay states requires the implementation of efficient systems has resulted in very few homeowners voluntarily adopting this technology.

Addressing nonpoint sources of nutrients, in general, has proved to be even more difficult than tackling point sources. The intensification of farming practices; the widespread use of fertilizers for residential use; the loss to development of natural buffers and wetlands; the paving of roads and urban areas; the increased number of cars on the road; and the substantial political clout that developers, realtors, car manufacturers, utility companies, and agricultural interests possess in the Bay states make achieving meaningful reductions from nonpoint sources of nutrients particularly difficult. While technologies exist to address each of these sources of nutrients, implementation often comes with a heavy price to government and the general public.

One of the most promising ways to reduce nonpoint source nutrient loading comes from agricultural best management practices (BMPs). The basic logic behind the practices is fairly straightforward. They aim to produce environmental gains by reducing the amount of nutrient-rich fertilizers applied to crops to the absolute minimum that is necessary to produce healthy crops. Moreover, they limit the amount of nutrients that leave agricultural areas by creating vegetation and forest buffers, using conservation tillage, and installing manure storage structures and manure runoff controls. Chapter 4 explores the political forces that tend to work against this and other nutrient-wise public policies.

THE SCORECARD: MEASURING
NUTRIENT REDUCTION "SUCCESS"

Accurately estimating trends in the amount of nutrients entering the Chesapeake Bay poses immense challenges to researchers and resource managers. Nutrients enter the Bay from countless sources throughout the 64,000-square-mile area that comprises the Bay's watershed and the 418,000-square-mile area that makes up the Bay's "air shed."[26] The size of the area and the number of sources contributing nutrients to the Bay make monitoring based on the direct observation of nutrient inputs impossible. Consequently, researchers rely on two different measuring techniques: (1) monitoring based on samples collected from the Bay's tributaries and mainstem and (2) estimates derived from computer models to approximate the amount of nutrients entering the Bay.

Beyond the sheer size of the region, the artificial distinction between the "controllable" and "noncontrollable" nutrients that the Chesapeake Bay Program made between 1987 and 2000 significantly complicated calculating nutrient loads. Ostensibly, nutrient managers made this distinction so that the restoration program would be evaluated based on factors that are within human control. The basic idea is that it would be unreasonable to assess nutrient reduction efforts based on factors that are beyond human influence. Consequently, the Bay Program has relied heavily on computer models that estimate the amount of nutrients entering the Bay, excluding nutrients that come from uncontrollable sources. Nutrients that enter the Bay naturally from forests, nutrients that enter the Bay from the atmosphere, and nutrients derived from states that are not signatories of the Bay Agreement (i.e., West Virginia, New York, and Delaware) were classified as uncontrollable.[27]

While the desire to distinguish between controllable and uncontrollable nutrient sources is understandable, adopting this approach raises several controversies. Most important, the 1987 task force that arrived at the 40 percent nutrient reduction goal for restoring the Chesapeake Bay's water quality did not distinguish between controllable and uncontrollable sources of nutrients. That task force estimated that a 40 percent reduction in the total amount of nutrients entering the Bay was the minimum reduction necessary to bring about the desired improvements to the Bay's living resources. Based on the findings of the task force, the 1987 Bay Agreement also made no distinction between controllable and uncontrollable nutrients, setting as its primary goal to "achieve by the year 2000 at least a 40 percent reduction of nitrogen and phosphorus entering the main stem of the Chesapeake Bay." Despite the call for at least a 40 percent reduction of all the nitrogen and phosphorus polluting the Bay, the Chesapeake Bay Program and its restoration partners interpreted the 1987 goal as merely reducing 40 percent of "controllable" nutrients.[28] As a consequence, had reduction efforts been "successful," they would have only reduced the amount of nitrogen entering the Bay by about 25 percent and the amount of phosphorus by 22 percent and would have failed to achieve the desired environmental impact.[29]

It should also be noted that many of the factors identified by the Bay Program as uncontrollable between years 1987 and 2000 are in fact well within human control. For example, nitrogen loading from the atmosphere, which was until recently classified as an uncontrollable nutrient source by the Chesapeake Bay Program, a nutrient source known to account for roughly a quarter of the nitrogen entering the Bay, is primarily the result of controllable human activities (i.e., a by-product of combustion engines).[30] Similarly, it has been misleading to classify nutrients entering from states that are nonsignatories of the Bay Agreement as uncontrollable. While nutrient loading from these states might be less controlled than from states that have signed the agreement, they are no less controllable in a scientific sense and their effects are no less deleterious to the Bay.

Another consequence of distinguishing between controllable and uncontrollable nutrients is that it has led to the heavy reliance on computer models (statistically derived estimations), rather than direct monitoring to assess the success of restoration programs. The computer models can be thought of as a complex accounting system in which the 64,000-square-mile watershed is broken down into smaller subwatersheds. Each of the smaller watersheds is then further broken down into land usage types (e.g., forested, urban, pasture, cropland, residential land, and so on).[31] Computer models estimate the amount of nutrients entering the Bay by combining land usage data from across the watershed with estimations of the amount of nutrients that typically come from each land usage type.[32] The models have appeal to Bay managers because they allow for predictions of how a change in land use (e.g., placing a certain amount of agricultural land under BMPs) might reduce nutrient loading to the Bay. Models also allow for noncontrollable nutrient sources to be removed from consideration.

Several problems are associated with relying extensively on computer-based estimations rather than monitoring. At the very least, the numerous assumptions built into the computer models may limit the validity of the findings.[33] That is, each assumption within the model carries with it a degree of uncertainty (i.e., error), regardless of the sophistication of the model. When layer upon layer of assumptions are built into highly complex statistical models, even small errors can substantially alter the findings. The practice is as problematic as trying to predict weather conditions or economic conditions a year in advance. While our understanding of these issues might lead to computer models that give us some insights into future conditions, the complexity of these phenomena assure that computer estimations never fully capture the processes. The combined result of applying several layers of assumptions is that at the end of the day a computer model may only roughly measure the concept in question.

Environmental scientists have begun to grow wary of the Bay Program's heavy reliance on computer modeling. President of the University of Maryland Center for Environmental Science, Dr. Don Boesch, explains that the Bay Program's models "have been relatively isolated from the kind of ongoing scientific criticism and evaluation that could make them more effective." Boesch and other scientists have argued that modeling and monitoring are most valuable when they are well integrated. He argues, "One of the problems with the Chesapeake Bay Program is that they have not been [integrated]. The environment is so complex you need to make observations, and you need to be prepared by surprises and learn from them."[34]

The ultimate threat of distinguishing between controllable and noncontrollable nutrients and relying on computer estimations rather than direct monitoring is that it can lead to misleading findings. Mike Hirshfield, vice president of resource protection at the Chesapeake Bay Foundation from 1996 to 2001, has expressed concern that the optimistic assumptions built into the Chesapeake Bay Program's computer models have substantially overestimated the amount of nutrients being reduced from nonpoint sources.[35] Dr. Tom Simpson (2002), the chair of the Bay Program's Nutrient Subcommittee, acknowledges that the models "assume complete implementation and perfect maintenance" of nutrient control practices, virtually guaranteeing that the models overestimate nutrient reduction efforts.

Reliance on models allowed the Bay Program to report from 1997 through early 2000 that the Bay states were on track to achieve the 40 percent reduction goal set in 1987 for phosphorus and that they were close to meeting the goal for nitrogen, a claim that was echoed throughout the media.[36] This encouraging news led many people to incorrectly assume that approximately 40 percent less nutrients were entering the Bay in the year 2000 than entered the Bay in 1985. Since approximately half of the Bay's nitrogen and phosphorus had been deemed uncontrollable, the actual reduction in nutrients entering the Bay was far less than 40 percent. In fact, the Bay Program now concedes that it failed to achieve even its modified reduction goals for controllable nutrients. By its own computer estimates, the Bay Program fell 2.3 million pounds per year short of its goal for controllable phosphorus and 24 million pounds per year shy of its controllable nitrogen goal.[37]

The U.S. Geological Survey (USGS) of nutrient trends for the Chesapeake Bay (1985–1999), trends that are based on direct monitoring rather than computer estimates, reveals even less optimistic findings than those presented by the Bay Program. The U.S. Geological Survey analyzes nutrient trends from thirty-one locations throughout the Bay watershed and reports trends for both total nitrogen and total phosphorus. The USGS study found that between 1985 and 1999 there was no significant reduction in the total nitrogen and total phosphorus loads at the majority of the thirty-one sites tested. For nitrogen, there was no significant change at 27 of the sites, while 2 sites measured a significant decrease,[38] and 2 sites measured a significant increase.[39] For phosphorus, there was no significant change at 25 of the 31 sites, with significant reductions at 5 sites,[40] and a significant increase at 1 site.[41]

It is important to note that stream flow rates, which are known to be positively related to nutrient loading,[42] did not generally experience upward trends at most of the monitored USGS sites during this period—only 4 of the 31 sights had significant flow increases from 1985 to 1999, with only 1 of the sites recording a significant increase in its nutrient load as well as a significant increase in flow rate.[43] Therefore, the general lack of nutrient reductions and the increases in nutrient loads at the identified sites cannot be explained away as the consequence of naturally occurring increases in river flows over this period of time, since for the most part there were no significant upward trends in river flows between 1985 and 1999.[44] Dr. Hirshfield (2002) explains, "If there was a significant increase in flow, then you would definitely have to take that into account. If there is just a lot of noise in the flow, then for the nutrient to be reduced to an amount that might actually make a difference in the Bay, it ought to be able to overcome that noise."

Given the difficulties of estimating nutrient loading in the Bay and its tributaries, it is worthwhile to explore alternative means for assessing trends in the Bay's nutrient loads. Karlsen et al. (2000) published an innovative study that helps illuminate the historical effects of nutrient loads in the Bay. Karlsen and his colleagues used biological records taken from sediment cores in the Bay to track the effects of oxygen depletion, one of the most harmful consequences of nutrient loading. From the core samples, they found evidence that oxygen depletion spiked during the 1970s and has not substantially declined since this period.[45] Similar sediment core studies (Cooper and Brush 1991; Cooper 1995) add further weight to the argument that nutrient loading trends, at least the deleterious effects from nutrient loading, has not significantly changed in recent years. Moreover, the abundance of underwater grasses, the living resource that first led researchers to question the long-term effects of nutrient loading in the Bay, has not rebounded in recent years, as would be expected if water quality had improved throughout the Bay.[46]

CONCLUSION

While the exact level of nutrient loading in the Chesapeake Bay can be debated indefinitely, the fact remains that the overall effort to improve the water quality of the Bay, so as to achieve a corresponding improvement in the abundance of the Bay's living resources, has not succeeded. Nutrient reduction efforts remain a means to an unrealized end—the improvement of the life-supporting ability of the Bay. This chapter suggests that scientific research has clearly identified the problem and has produced innovations that could reduce the problem if more fully implemented. The issue today does not represent a scientific problem, but a political problem. That is, how to persuade industry leaders, policymakers, and average citizens to adopt difficult and potentially costly public policy choices so that the Bay may in fact improve. The following chapter of this study investigates the political forces that work to constrain environmental success.

4

The Political Fight for Nutrient Management Policy

The Case of Agricultural Regulation

The fundamental problem is the source, and that is getting farmers to adopt these practices. . . . Thus we must ask: Are voluntary programs which encourage, but do not require, the installation of agricultural best management practices sufficient to stem the flow of nutrients and sediments leaving our farmlands and entering our waterways, or are regulatory measures called for?

—Chesapeake Bay Commission (1985), *Annual Report to the General Assemblies of Maryland, Pennsylvania, and Virginia*

The goal of reducing the Bay's nitrogen and phosphorus by 40 percent by 2000 has not yet been met. There is now clear recognition that restoring water quality to a "clean Bay" status will require even further reductions—perhaps double, if not triple, the reductions already accomplished.

—Chesapeake Bay Commission (2001b), *Seeking Solutions: Chesapeake Bay Commission, Annual Report*

The political struggle to curtail the flow of unwanted nutrient waste into the Chesapeake Bay can be traced back over a century. In 1862, the Baltimore Sewage Commission issued a report in which it considered the dangers of releasing large amounts of untreated sewage into the Bay's tributaries, as was the practice at the time.[1] Public concern regarding the noxious odors emanating from the Bay's waters around urban centers like Baltimore, Washington, and Hampton Roads spiked in 1893 when scientists made a direct link between typhoid fever and the consumption of oysters contaminated by human waste.[2] Typhoid outbreaks in Chicago, New York, and Washington during the winter of 1924, which killed 150 people, further increased public concerns over the long-term consequences of flushing untreated waste into bodies of water like the Chesapeake Bay.[3]

More than a century has passed since scientists began reporting the human health and environmental dangers associated with human waste, and the Bay is perhaps further from solving its nutrient management problems today than it was a century ago.[4] Major headlines in 2002 tell of massive sewage leaks and spills in the Baltimore area (i.e., Jones Falls, Gwynns Falls, and Herring Run) and along tributaries of the Potomac, resulting in the release of over five million gallons of untreated waste into the Bay and its tributaries.[5] As many of the area's major sewage treatment systems grow outdated and inefficient, these sewage spills have become regular occurrences in many parts of the watershed.

Today, nutrient management entails far more than simply treating human waste in a manner that does not foul the water and cause human illness, though these issues remain pressing concerns. Modern nutrient management entails nothing less than changing the way we live our lives, the way we develop the land, and the basic manner in which we interact with our surroundings. Modern nutrient management is multi-faceted and includes diverse considerations such as enforcing phosphate detergent bans, applying biological nutrient removal technology to sewage treatment, updating septic systems, increasing emission control technologies for cars and utility companies, developing animal waste enzyme technologies, curbing urban growth, promoting public transportation, improving storm water runoff systems, protecting natural forest buffers, and implementing agricultural best management practices (BMPs).[6] It is a massive, high-stakes undertaking that will, more than any other factor, determine the environmental health of the Chesapeake Bay and its tributaries in the years to come.

In this limited study, a comprehensive exploration of the politics of nutrient reduction, with its multiple facets, is impractical. Instead, this chapter focuses on the politics of controlling one key aspect of nutrient pollution—that is, the politics of environmental regulations for agricultural production. The study gives special attention to the agricultural policies of Maryland and Pennsylvania, since these two states are widely considered leaders in agricultural nutrient management among the Bay states. Exploring nutrient management through the study's theoretical lens reveals how economic considerations, the nation's fragmented political structure, interest group competition, and focusing events play important roles in the politics of agricultural management.

AGRICULTURAL NUTRIENT LOADING

The harm of agricultural pollutants to the Chesapeake Bay has been well established. The Environmental Protection Agency's original seven-year study of the Chesapeake Bay ecosystem concluded that nonpoint source nutrient loading, much of which has been linked to agricultural production, was among the chief factors responsible for the Bay's deterioration.[7] More recent studies have reinforced this finding, estimating that nonpoint sources of nutrients contribute as much as 68 percent of the phosphorus and 77 percent of the nitrogen entering the Bay.[8] While nonpoint sources of nutrients enter the Bay in numerous ways, not just from agriculture, agricultural runoff from cropland, pastureland, and animal waste has been identified as the single largest source of these pollutants. The Chesapeake Bay Program estimates that 58 percent of the nonpoint source nitrogen and 82 percent of the nonpoint source phosphorus that pollutes the Bay are the by-products of agriculture production.[9] This level of nutrient loading is even more remarkable considering that agricultural land comprises only 29 percent of the Chesapeake Bay drainage basin.[10]

Farm production, absent of menacing pipes and unsightly smoke-stacks, has been described as the Bay's silent killer. Behind its bucolic veil, modern farming practices utilize immense quantities of fertilizer and produce massive amounts of animal waste, doing more harm to the Chesapeake Bay than any other factor. In some of the watershed's most beautiful areas, such as Pennsylvania's Lancaster County, Virginia's Shenandoah Valley, and Maryland's Eastern Shore, large animal operations produce enormous amounts of nutrients that pollute the Bay. One study estimated that Lancaster County alone produces as much as 5 million tons (i.e., 10 billion pounds) of animal waste per year.[11] These agriculturally intense areas, with their relatively small human populations, produce as much biological waste from their livestock as humans produce in midsized cities.

Unlike human waste, however, there are no sewage treatment plants to control and mitigate the environmental impact of poultry, dairy, and swine production. Animal manure has traditionally been applied to cropland as a natural fertilizer, returning to the soil essential nutrients that are removed with each harvest. As animal production has intensified and cropland has been lost to development, the amount of natural fertilizer produced from animal production has come to surpass the fertilizer needs of many areas in the watershed. The region's animal waste surplus creates a strong incentive for farmers to overfertilize their crops. Since fertilizer needs are linked to weather conditions that cannot be accurately predicted, the precise fertilizer requirements of a crop are uncertain. With fertilizer costs relatively low, the natural tendency is to overestimate the fertilizer needs of a crop and, consequently, to overfertilize fields. The excess nutrients that result from overfertilization eventually find their way to the Bay either as cropland runoff or through groundwater.

Nutrient loading from agriculture poses a daunting challenge to the Chesapeake Bay restoration effort. It has been estimated that agricultural waste is responsible for more of the Bay's phosphorus and nitrogen load than the combined nutrient loads from urban runoff, all point sources, septic systems, and the atmosphere—contributing more than 110 million pounds of nitrogen and 9 million pounds of phosphorus to the Bay per year. In comparison, the estimated annual nutrient load from all point sources, industrial sources and sewage treatment plants included, is about 60 million pounds of nitrogen and 4.4 million pounds of phosphorus.[12] It is now clear that unless the problem of agricultural waste is adequately addressed, the overall effort to restore the Bay is unlikely to succeed.

While the amount of pollution produced from modern agricultural practices is considerable, it is by no means uncontrollable. Table 4.1 outlines several innovative agricultural best management practices (BMPs) that could, if fully implemented, substantially reduce the negative impact of agricultural production. The logic behind each of these practices is fairly straightforward. Each of the agricultural BMPs is designed to reduce the negative impact of agricultural runoff by either limiting the amount of nutrients that are applied to agricultural lands (e.g., fertilizer management practices) or by creating storage, buffering, and filtering systems that minimize the amount of nutrients that move from agricultural land to the Chesapeake Bay and its tributaries. Another approach that is being explored is the use of animal waste as fuel for the production of electricity, which could potentially eliminate large quantities of nutrients, provide the region with a renewable energy source, and help to correct fertilizer prices.

In a 1995 report, the Chesapeake Bay Program estimated that implementing environmentally wise farm management practices could eliminate 38 million pounds of nitrogen from entering the Bay each year.[13] A more recent analysis completed by the Chesapeake Bay Program estimated that fully implementing environmentally sound agricultural management practices could remove as much as 100 million pounds of nitrogen from entering the Bay per year.[14] In other words, agricultural BMPs could reduce more than a third of the annual nonpoint source nitrogen entering the Bay and would have the equivalent impact of eliminating the Bay's entire point source nutrient load.[15] Given the amount of nutrients entering the Bay as

Table 4.1. Common Agricultural Best Management Practices (BMPs)

Forested Buffers	Maintain a strip of forests along rivers and streams to filter nutrients.
Grassed Buffers	Maintain a strip of grass along rivers and streams to filter nutrients.
Cover Crops	Plant small grain plants without fertilizer in September and early October on land otherwise fallow. The practice reduces nitrate leaching and erosion.
Conservation Tillage	Seed crops directly into vegetation cover or crop residue so as to minimize soil disturbance, erosion, and nutrient loss to surrounding bodies of water.
Contour Farming	Tilling soil perpendicular to the slope of the land or creating terraces so as to reduce soil and nutrient loss.
Fertilizer Management Plans	Implement plans that manage the amount, timing, and placement of fertilizer and animal waste on crops.
Retirement of Erodible Land	Remove from production lands that are highly susceptible to erosion due to geographic conditions.
Stream Protection with Fencing	Restrict livestock access to streams and rivers by fencing or creating water troughs away from streams to limit nutrient loading associated with livestock waste.
Animal Waste Systems	Implement systems for handling and storing waste generated by confined animals (i.e., livestock and poultry), such as storage lagoons, ponds, or tanks.

Sources: Reproduced by author from Maryland Nutrient Cap Workgroup (2001, 20) and EPA (1988b, 78–85).

a consequence of agricultural production and the sizeable reductions that agricultural BMPs promise, many of the Bay's strongest advocates have been fighting for agricultural reforms for over two decades.

Unfortunately, there remains a wide gap between the potential benefits and the realized benefits from agricultural reform. For example, while there are nearly twelve million acres of cropland and pastureland in the Chesapeake basin,[16] agricultural management plans have only been developed for 35 percent of the Bay's agricultural land,[17] and the plans have been fully implemented for an even smaller portion of the Bay's agricultural land. The Chesapeake Bay Program estimates that nearly 70 percent of the Bay's agricultural nitrogen load could be eliminated through best management practices, though generous estimates put the annual nitrogen reduction from agriculture sources since 1985 at about 23 percent.[18] Policymakers throughout the watershed have relied heavily on voluntary educational programs and limited financial inducements to persuade farmers to adopt Bay-friendly farming practices. While this approach has led to the voluntary adoption of some environmentally wise agricultural practices, it has failed to bring about the far-reaching nutrient reductions that agricultural BMPs promise and that are necessary for the restoration of the Chesapeake Bay.

The question remains, given the known environmental problems associated with agricultural runoff and the known benefits that could be achieved by more fully implementing environmentally friendly farming techniques, why does agricultural production throughout the watershed remain a relatively unregulated industry that adds more pollutants to the Chesapeake Bay than any other source? To address this issue we must investigate the political forces that have led to the existing agricultural regulations, or in this case, lack of enforceable regulations. The following section outlines the fight for agricultural regulations in Pennsylvania and Maryland. The chapter concludes by exploring the issue through the study's theoretical lens.

POLITICAL BACKGROUND: THE FIGHT FOR ENFORCEABLE AGRICULTURAL REGULATIONS IN MARYLAND AND PENNSYLVANIA

Recognizing the negative impact of modern agricultural practices, the Chesapeake Bay Commission's first annual report, in 1981, "attributed most of the [Bay's] nitrogen from agricultural runoff" (D-13). Likewise, when the EPA released the results of its seven-year study of the Chesapeake Bay in 1983, it specifically identified agricultural runoff as a primary factor responsible for the Bay's decline. Neither report was particularly surprising to the scientific community, which had come to recognize the environmental hazards associated with modern agricultural practices. Section 208 of the Clean Water Act, passed in the early 1970s, recognized the impact of agriculture and required all states to identify sources of nutrient pollutants, including agricultural sources, and to develop strategies for addressing these problems.[19]

Even with the Clean Water Act's federal requirements for states to develop Section 208 plans and an extensive body of scientific evidence suggesting that nutrient waste from agriculture has caused serious harm to the Bay, Maryland and other Bay states have resisted implementing meaningful agricultural nutrient restrictions and have instead relied on educational outreach programs and underfunded government cost-share programs to entice farmers to voluntarily adopt nutrient management practices.[20] By the early 1980s, both Virginia and Maryland had Section 208 plans on the books, but neither state required nutrient management plans for agricultural producers, and neither state allocated substantial funding for environmental cost-sharing programs or other agricultural programs intended to protect the Bay.[21]

Maryland took the early lead in pushing for environmentally wise agricultural practices in 1987 when the state's governor, William Schaefer, and state's secretary of agriculture, Wayne Cawley, set the ambitious goals of having all Maryland farmers voluntarily develop management plans within a decade and for every farm within a priority area to adopt plans within five years.[22] That same year, the governors of Maryland, Virginia, Pennsylvania, the mayor of the District of Columbia, the head of the EPA, and the director of the Chesapeake Bay Commission signed the 1987 Chesapeake Bay Agreement that set the even more ambitious goal of reducing by at least 40 percent the controllable nutrients entering the Bay by 2000. The general assumption that guided this Agreement and that fueled much of the Bay restoration effort since the early 1980s was that research, moral suasion, and education, combined with modest government support, would be sufficient to bring about the desired outcomes.

Unfortunately, without mandatory nutrient regulations in place for agriculture and sufficient funding for technical assistance and cost-share programs, the goals outlined in the various agreements have consistently come up short.[23] As early as 1985, the Chesapeake Bay Commission publicly questioned whether voluntary agricultural programs alone could succeed in bringing about the desired large-scale reductions in nonpoint source nutrients needed for Bay restoration.[24] By 1990, the Chesapeake Bay Non-Point Source Program Evaluation Panel (1990), a broad-based independent panel convened by the EPA, concluded that the Bay Program's nutrient reduction goals were unlikely to be met through voluntary nonpoint source programs. The panel concluded that the states and federal government should "augment voluntary programs with increased use of regulatory authority for the reduction of nutrient loadings" (7). That same year, a select committee convened by Governor Bob Casey of Pennsylvania concluded that regulatory measures were necessary for agriculture if the state was to meet its nutrient management goals.[25] These sentiments were reinforced in 1991 when the Chesapeake Bay Commission reported that the amount of nitrogen in the main stem of the Chesapeake Bay, much of which was coming from agriculture, had actually increased by 2 percent since 1985. Finally, in 1991, the Chesapeake Bay Commission publicly endorsed mandatory agricultural regulation as one means of addressing nutrient loading.

After two years of internal debate and an extensive analysis by Governor Casey's select committee, Pennsylvania became the first Bay state to introduce legislation mandating agricultural management plans for its farmers (House Bill 496) during its 1991–1992 legislative session.[26] With strong opposition from farm organizations, agribusinesses, and Republicans who controlled the state senate at the time, the legislation was killed during the 1991–1992 session. After Democrats took control of the Pennsylvania Senate in 1992, establishing control of both chambers, a compromise version of the legislation was passed in 1993 (House Bill 100) that called on the state Conservation Commission, guided by a Nutrient Management Advisory Board, to draft agricultural management regulations within two years (by 1995). The law also called for farmers to develop nutrient management plans within one year of the regulations (by 1996) and for farm operations to implement nutrient plans, with state assistance, within three years of submitting plans (by 1999).

Passage of the 1993 legislation did not end the debate regarding mandatory agriculture management plans for Pennsylvania's agricultural industry. Republicans regained control of the General Assembly and the governor's office in 1994 and were able to delay the promulgation of agricultural regulations until 1997, two years after the deadline established by the 1993 law. Not only were farming interests able to stall implementation of the law, they were able to greatly influence the regulations that eventually emerged. The regulations that were issued in 1997 only applied to high-density animal operations that comprise somewhere between 5 and 10 percent of Pennsylvania farms and provided loopholes that further weakened the law. Farm organizations had diluted the regulations to the point that former supporters of the 1993 legislation, groups like the Chesapeake Bay Foundation, were forced to publicly criticize the regulations and to question whether the law, as interpreted by the commission, would help to meaningfully control agricultural nutrient loads from the state.[27] Pennsylvania's decade-long push for the implementation of mandatory nutrient management plans for its farming community has yet to be realized for the majority of its farmland.

In 1992, Maryland State Senator Gerald Winegrad, a strong advocate for the Bay, introduced legislation to the Maryland General Assembly that would have required Maryland farmers to implement best management practices by no later than 2000. Facing even stronger opposition within the farming community than was the case in Pennsylvania, the legislative push to move to mandatory farm management plans in Maryland was defeated in the 1992, 1993, and 1994 legislative sessions. Had it not been for the 1997 *Pfiesteria* outbreak that shocked the state into action, mandatory BMP legislation may not have been considered again in Maryland.

Following the *Pfiesteria* outbreak, the 1998 Maryland legislative assembly managed to produce a bill that melded an industry-friendly bill, introduced by Ron Guns, the conservative chairman of the House Environmental Matters Committee,[28] with a stronger environmental bill supported by Governor Parris Glendening and State Senator Brian Frosh. The law that emerged was widely touted as the most comprehensive agricultural nutrient management legislation in the country. The 1998 Water Quality Improvement Act gave Maryland farmers until the end of 2001 to develop mandatory nitrogen management plans and required that they comply with the plans by the end of 2002. Unlike the Pennsylvania law, which applied to only a small number of large farm operations, the Maryland law applied to all but the smallest farm operations in the state.[29] Moreover, the law established sizeable penalties for noncompliance that would be applied following a warning period.

Unfortunately, the Maryland law, like the Pennsylvania law before it, has had little impact on farm management practices. At the beginning of 2002, some thirty years after passage of the federal Clean Water Act, fifteen years after Maryland Governor Schaefer set his goal for conservation plans, three years after the Maryland General Assembly passed its much-touted Water Quality Improvement Act, and after the deadline for nitrogen management plans had come and gone, data from the Maryland Department of Agriculture showed that only 20 percent of Maryland's 1.7 million acres of farmland were under nutrient management plans. Only 2,152 of the more than 7,000 farm operations in Maryland had submitted nutrient management plans. Nearly three thousand farm operations had filed delay forms, and the remainder of farm operations had not filed any of the required forms. Quite simply, the majority of farm operations had either ignored the law or grown frustrated with Maryland's agricultural bureaucracy, which remains inadequate to meet its growing responsibilities. The fight for meaningful agricultural reform continues.

ENVIRONMENTAL THEORY: TOWARD A DEEPER UNDERSTANDING OF THE AGRICULTURAL REGULATION FIGHT

In both Maryland and Pennsylvania, well-intentioned advocates, from within and outside of government, have worked hard to pass agricultural regulations for the Bay. Even with a scientific consensus regarding the impact of agriculture and with the general public strongly supporting policy for the Bay, neither state has come close to successfully addressing its agricultural problems. The following analysis helps to explain *why* agricultural reform has proved to be such a difficult political problem. Here we apply the study's theory (figure 4.1) and see how economic factors, interest group opposition, and intergovernmental competition can coalesce to stifle agricultural regulation, and how events within the policy cycle create fleeting opportunities for policy innovation.

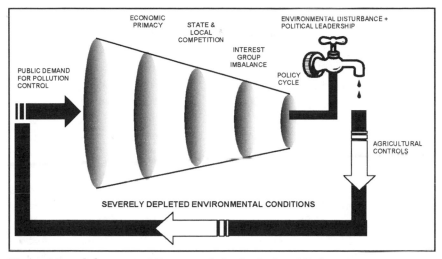

Figure 4.1.   A Conceptual Framework for Agricultural Reform
Graphic design by Christine Jamison.

ECONOMIC PRIMACY AND AGRICULTURAL POLICY FOR THE BAY

For the three signatory states of the Bay Agreements, Maryland, Virginia, and Pennsylvania, the agricultural industry remains a powerful economic force that is well represented throughout government. In these states, agricultural production grosses over $6 billion per year—Maryland, $1.4 billion; Virginia, $2.4 billion; and Pennsylvania, $4 billion. Pennsylvania's fifty-nine thousand farms help to make agriculture the state's leading industry.[30]

While the industry remains relatively diverse across the three states, poultry production reigns supreme in Maryland and Virginia, with an annual production of over 500 million chickens and a gross income over $700 million per year. Chicken production is also large in Pennsylvania, producing over 100 million chickens annually, but dairy is Pennsylvania's chief agricultural commodity.[31] The productivity of Pennsylvania's top dairying counties (i.e., Lancaster, Franklin, Bradford, and Berks) helps to make Pennsylvania the fourth largest milk-producing state in the nation. Agriculture production and its related industries form a multi-billion-dollar economic force in the Bay states, stretching over eleven million acres and having a substantial presence in every region of the watershed.

For the agricultural industry, nutrient management regulations are first and foremost a financial issue. While some advocates of agricultural reform suggest that environmentally sensitive agricultural practices might be achieved at little or no expense to agribusiness, the reluctance within the farming industry to voluntarily adopt such practices suggests that the farming community does not generally agree. A study completed by Penn State researchers in the late 1980s supports this belief, estimating that fully adopting the environmental management practices of the day would likely cost a typical dairy farm 20 percent of its income.[32] A more recent study conducted by the Environmental Protection Agency's Chesapeake Bay Program in 1995 estimated that it would likely cost around $372 million for agriculture to implement nonpoint source nutrient controls across the watershed.[33]

These relatively low estimates do not generally represent one-time expenses. Many of the costs of environmentally friendly farm practices, such as low tillage, cover crops, and fertilizer reductions, accrue annually. Likewise, other controls, like farm plans and animal waste controls, must be updated on a regular basis. And promising new approaches that were not considered in earlier studies, such as "yield reserve" practices that provide insurance to farmers who reduce fertilizer application and "manure-to-power" programs that turn animal waste into electricity, could substantially increase the annual cost of agricultural controls.

The economic impact of agricultural nutrient controls complicates the politics of nutrient reduction, forcing state officials to weigh the potential benefits of environmental reforms against the known cost of such measures. As discussed earlier, the regulatory approach, which puts the financial burden directly on the agricultural industry, has politically been the most difficult course of action. This approach calls on political actors, many representing rural areas and almost all having agricultural interests among their constituents, to place financial burdens on what might be the leading industry and primary employer in their districts. Aware of the potential political fallout from such action, none of the Bay states have effectively pursued this course of action.

The alternative approach is to provide financial inducements for farmers to voluntarily adopt nutrient reduction controls. While each state has been willing to commit modest amounts of public funds to encourage environmentally sensitive agricultural practices, and the farming community has generally proved willing to implement such programs if given sufficient funding, none of the Bay states have been able to muster sufficient resources to bring about the widespread implementation of nutrient controls called for under the Bay Agreements through financial inducements alone.

In the fiercely competitive world of budgetary politics, funding agricultural programs has a political cost of its own, though perhaps a lower cost than pursuing agricultural regulations. Pursuing financial inducements requires elected officials to appropriate limited public funds to agricultural producers—many of which are major corporations or contractors of major corporations. Since the available funds are limited, this subsidy inevitably comes at the expense of other government services, which are often deemed more essential than agricultural subsidies. Moreover, it is not surprising that during periods of economic downturn, which are often felt deepest at the state level, states tend to cut back money allocated to agricultural programs in order to protect more popular government programs.

THE INTEREST GROUP IMBALANCE
AND AGRICULTURAL POLICY FOR THE BAY

The interest group imbalance between the groups that represent the agricultural industry and environmental groups is clearly evident in the Bay states. As Olson and others would predict (see chapter 2), the Chesapeake Bay Foundation and the other pro-environment groups in the area, with their broad environmental agenda and pursuit of public goods, simply cannot compete with the political machinery that comprises the agribusiness lobby in the Bay states. The area's agricultural interests are presented by a large network of well-financed interest groups, which are actively involved in every aspect of the political process.

Chief among these groups is the American Farm Bureau, which has grown from its modest beginnings in 1919 into a massive organization that boasts the membership of over five million members nationwide. The Farm Bureau maintains a team of registered lobbyists at the federal level, as well as an active lobbying presence in its state affiliates, including each of the Bay states. The Maryland Farm Bureau alone has a full-time government relations staff comparable to the entire lobbying arm of the Chesapeake Bay Foundation, which represents a broad spectrum of environmental issues across six states and within the federal government.

Unlike the Chesapeake Bay Foundation, the Maryland, Virginia, and Pennsylvania Farm Bureaus each operate active political action committees (PACs), which make financial contributions to political candidates. The Virginia Farm Bureau also publicly endorses political candidates, a level of political activity that the Chesapeake Bay Foundation and many other environmental groups have avoided.

Beyond the farm bureaus, there are a host of industry-specific groups that fight to protect farmers from costly environmental regulations. In Maryland alone, more than a dozen agricultural associations have come together to create a formidable coalition that has dubbed itself "The Coalition to Improve Nutrient Management." Member groups in this coalition include Maryland Farm Bureau, Maryland Grain Producers Association, Maryland Pork Producers Association, Delmarva Poultry Industry, Maryland Nursery and Landscape Association, Maryland State Grange, Maryland Dairy Industry Association, Association of Soil Conservation Districts, Delaware–Maryland Agribusiness Association, Maryland Cattlemen's Association, and Maryland Sheep Breeders Association.[34] Beyond the efforts of the coalition, many of these groups maintain government relations staffs of their own and contribute to political campaigns through political action committees, further augmenting the influence of the agricultural industry.

An important political force within the agricultural community that is often overlooked is the influence of individual farming families. Unlike typical family farmers who generally shun politics, the farming dynasties behind major agricultural operations such as the Tyson Foods, Perdue Farms, and Allen Family Foods are often active political actors at the state and local levels. For example, a single agricultural family, the Perdue family, spent more in one recent election cycle in support of Maryland candidates than the combined spending of all environmental groups across the three key Bay states during the same period.[35] Families like Perdue offer sizeable aggregate contributions by dividing their contributions among multiple family members and contributing to several candidates. These families can also exert influence on the political process in less public ways, such as hosting fund-raisers for political candidates or making contributions to industry associations.

According to the National Institute on Money in State Politics (2002), agricultural interests in Maryland, Pennsylvania, and Virginia outspent environmental groups in recent elections $910,000 to $7,000.[36] Moreover, it is important to note that the disparity only represents one aspect of the interest group imbalance between and environmental groups. The agricultural industry as a whole also employs a larger number of professional lobbyists and spends more on public relations efforts than environmental groups in the area. The Maryland Farm Bureau alone reported spending more than $64,000 in lobbying expenses in the year 2000.[37] All told, the agricultural industry's large population base, robust financial backing, and willingness to engage in the political process combine to make it a powerful political force.

While there exists a substantial disparity between agricultural and environmental groups, these figures do not suggest that environmental groups are entirely excluded from the debate over agricultural reform. On the contrary, environmental groups actively testify at public hearings and before the various general assemblies, often at rates greater than their industry counterparts. Moreover, they engage in traditional lobbying activities such as coalition building, grassroots mobilization, education of elected officials, and assistance of environmentally friendly officials. Nevertheless, its political naïveté and reluctance to actively participate in electoral politics ensures that the environmental community enters the process as an outsider, trying to achieve through the strength of its argument what industry advocates have already gained through more aggressive techniques.

DIVIDED GOVERNMENT AND
AGRICULTURAL POLICY FOR THE BAY

The Bay's agricultural industry has long benefited from the competitive forces that are fostered by the nation's fragmented political structure. At the state level, competition to attract and satisfy agricultural giants, such as Tyson and Perdue, causes states to think twice before enacting nutrient regulations that may repel these powerful interests. Large poultry producers and processors maintain operations in several states and are not tied by necessity to a particular state or region, allowing them to choose areas that provide a pro-industry climate and to move from areas where regulations become too costly. Companies like Tyson Foods contract out local farmers to produce the bulk of its chickens, rather than operating its own livestock operations. Tyson supplies the animals and feed and relies on local farmers to provide the necessary labor and facilities. This arrangement greatly reduces the corporation's capital costs and makes its operations mobile should the need to move arise.

The pressure to protect agricultural interests is often felt the strongest at the local level where agriculture has the ability to dominate a region's economy and politics. Examples of agriculturally intense areas are spread throughout the watershed, but are particularly prevalent in areas along Maryland's Eastern Shore, Virginia's Shenandoah Valley, and the areas around Lancaster County, Pennsylvania. Agriculture dominates the political and economic life of such places as Caroline County on the Delmarva Peninsula of Maryland's Eastern Shore, where over 54 percent of the county's land is used for agricultural production and agriculture is one of the chief sources of jobs for the county's thirty thousand residents. Likewise, agricultural interests are powerful in such places as Rockingham County, Virginia, where agriculture-related industries annually provide the county with more than $400 million in cash receipts.[38] Perhaps the most agriculturally intense area in the watershed is Lancaster County, Pennsylvania. This county leads the state in the production of cattle, chickens, and hogs, supporting nearly six thousand farms on more than 400,000 acres.[39]

It is important to note that in many of these agriculturally intense areas, such as Rockingham and Lancaster Counties, the Bay is a distant concern. These counties, like dozens of other agriculturally intense counties, are "upstream" areas that possess no Bay frontage of their own to protect, but are nevertheless in the Bay watershed. The expectation that local officials will actively seek or aggressively enforce environmental restrictions on agricultural production in these areas is simply unrealistic.

THE POLICY CYCLE, FOCUSING EVENTS, AND POLITICAL LEADERS: MAKING THE MOST OF LIMITED OPPORTUNITIES FOR AGRICULTURAL REFORM

Had the move to impose agricultural restrictions happened in the early 1980s, when hopes were high and conditions ripe for environmental action in the Bay states, perhaps greater gains would have been achieved than has been the case. During the early period in the restoration effort, the period that Downs describes as the "alarmed discovery and euphoric enthusiasm stage" (see chapter 2), the Bay's advocates chose a more cautious course for agricultural policy, pushing for voluntary agricultural reform rather than mandatory regulations. It was not until a decade later, in a political climate that had grown considerably less friendly for environmental regulations and after the voluntary approach had proved ineffective at producing widespread agricultural changes, that the political push for mandatory agricultural regulations began to take shape. By this time the restoration effort had moved into its "post-problem stage," a realm defined by lower expectations and sporadic public attention, where periodic events, not thoughtful planning, tend to fuel environmental public policy.

It was precisely such a focusing event that enabled advocates for farm regulations to temporarily gain the upper hand and win passage of mandatory agriculture regulations for the state of Maryland in 1998. As discussed earlier, an area of intense agricultural production along Maryland's Eastern Shore experienced widespread fish kills that attracted intense media attention in 1997. On August 6 and again on August 26, 1997, two substantial fish kills were reported in the Pocomoke area, the latest in a series of kills that had been reported throughout the summer. Crews from Maryland's Department of Natural Resources and Department of the Environment collected samples at the sites and concluded that the kills were related to toxic levels of *Pfiesteria,* an algae form associated with nutrient-polluted waters. A number of factors combined to heighten media attention and public concern: (1) *Pfiesteria* was a new problem for the Bay that had never before been addressed by resource managers; (2) the crisis affected important commercial industries (i.e., the commercial fishing industry, restaurant industry, and tourist industry); and (3) the problem raised human health concerns for which there were no clear answers.

The 1997 outbreak sparked Maryland governor, Parris Glendening, to call a Governors Summit in September 1997, bringing together political leaders from the six Bay states to discuss the crisis and to plan a coordinated course of action. Following the summit, Governor Glendening established his Blue Ribbon *Pfiesteria* Commission, chaired by former Maryland Governor Harry Hughes, a long-time champion of environmental policy in Maryland. This committee was tasked with studying the issue and presenting recommendations to Governor Glendening by November of that year. A Technical Advisory Committee was also formed to help determine the cause of the fish kills and to suggest a scientifically grounded plan to address the problem. Donald Boesch, president and professor at University of Maryland's Center for Environmental Science, was appointed to head Glendening's Technical Advisory Committee.

Lacking sufficient evidence to establish a direct connection between *Pfiesteria* and agricultural runoff with scientific certainty, Dr. Boesch and his committee were initially reluctant to attribute the outbreak to agricultural practices. Former Governor Hughes, aware of the importance of achieving a scientific consensus, prodded Boesch and his committee to report whatever consensus was possible. The report that emerged from the technical committee acknowledged that while there were many possible explanations for the *Pfiesteria* outbreak that caused the Pocomoke fish kills, nonpoint source nutrients from agriculture production was most likely the primary culprit and should receive the most attention. Hughes and his committee were able to make use of the scientific report to build a case for increased control of agricultural production. Governor Glendening in turn approved $2 million in emergency funding to pay farmers to plant cover crops and began to push for legislation that would require Maryland farmers to develop and implement nutrient management plans within a given period of time. The legislation that passed in the closing hours of the 1998 legislative session was the Water Quality Improvement Act of 1998. In many respects, the legislation was nearly identical to the agricultural regulations that Maryland State Senator Gerald Winegrad had unsuccessfully pushed for six years earlier in a different political context.

CONCLUSION

Proponents of agricultural reform are forced to traverse a difficult political terrain. It is a political landscape in which economic concerns, interest group pressure, and intergovernmental competition combine to create impressive obstacles for environmental policy innovation. For over two decades, these forces have worked against environmental advocates, scientific evidence, and the concerns of the general public. The obstacles to reform have left the governmental process unwilling, or perhaps incapable, of producing policies that adequately address the Bay's primary environmental hazard—agricultural pollution. The process has failed to produce enforceable regulations or to provide adequate funding to induce agricultural change. The politics of political expediency has moved forward slowly, producing a trickle of suboptimum agricultural policies that have failed to generate substantial environmental improvements.

Part III

THE BLUE CRAB
AND BAY POLITICS

5

All You Can Eat?

The Difficult Task of Protecting the Blue Crab

To get grasses back, to get oysters on the rebound, to maintain rockfish, to get crabs not on the edge but that can sustain an important recreational and commercial lifeblood of the Chesapeake, to bring back shad, perhaps not to the numbers we saw in the 1800s, but something that gives a fishery to Pennsylvania, D.C. and the Eastern Shore—it is going to take another big, big step.

—Richard Batiuk (2002), associate director for
science at the Chesapeake Bay Program

We lost the chance to act—for the first time in Bay history—in advance of a drastic decline; lost the chance to put crabbing on a sustainable basis before the threat of collapse forces harsher, less-considered actions.

—Tom Horton (2002b), columnist and author

Crabs from the Chesapeake have been contributing to the cultural, economic, and culinary richness of the region for well over a century. Reports of people eating crabs in the area date back to 1730 when William Byrd wrote of his experience eating a "flat crab" the size of his hand.[1] By the mid-1800s, the fleshy white meat of the blue crab was growing in popularity, with soft crabs leading the way as a much sought after delicacy. In 1836, Dr. John D. Godman, a Philadelphia physician, described soft crabs as "an exquisite treat by those who are fond of such eating."[2] By the 1870s, crab consumption had grown to the point that it sustained a small crabbing industry in Crisfield, Maryland, the birthplace of the Bay's commercial crabbing industry.

Today, the blue crab is the undisputed icon of the Chesapeake Bay. Each year church groups and community organizations from across the region gather to indulge in much-anticipated crab feasts. Picnic tables covered with brown paper and the clanking of wooden mallets have become the ubiquitous sights and sounds that define summers along the Chesapeake. For young people throughout the region, tying chicken necks to twine is far more than the method of choice for catching the blue crab; it is a cherished right of passage that has filled the summers of countless Virginians and Marylanders.[3] And for the hundreds of thousands of tourists who travel each year to Annapolis and other Bay hot spots, no trip is complete without at least one crab cake platter, or, for the more daring, a soft-shell sandwich.

For many of the Bay's approximately forty-eight hundred licensed commercial crabbers, colloquially known throughout the region as "watermen," harvesting crabs is a way of making a living that can be traced back several generations.[4] This difficult line of work supports unique communities in such places as Smith Island (Maryland), Crisfield (Maryland), and Tangier Island (Virginia) that appear to outsiders as if they were stuck in time.[5] The cultural richness and relative isolation of these areas are reflected in the distinct dialects that can be heard over marine radios throughout the Tangier/Pocomoke Sounds. One-syllable words like "tide" become multisyllabic utterances like "tee-i-ed," and the popular phrase "save the Bay-ers," a catchall phrase watermen use to describe the Bay's environmental advocates, is truncated to sound more like "save the bears." There are even subtle differences in dialects between island communities, enabling watermen to identify over the radio whether someone is from Tangier Island or Smith Island, which are located only a few miles apart.

Watermen communities tend to be pious, with church attendance high, and absence from Sunday service not only noticed, but also likely to raise sincere concerns within the congregation. Public drunkenness, a notorious problem in fishing communities in other areas of the country, is held in disdain in places like Tangier Island, where the sale of alcohol is prohibited. Strict community standards keep alcohol consumption relatively low and restricted to the private crab shacks that line the island's docks. Theirs is a way of life built on old-fashioned values and hard work that is as endangered as the ecosystem on which it is sustained.

The modern crabbing industry is also a robust economic force for the states of Virginia and Maryland. Historically, 50 percent of the country's hard crab harvest and 60 percent of the soft crab catch has come from the Chesapeake Bay. With the collapse of the Bay's oyster population, the blue crab fishery has increased in importance and is now the dominant commercial fishery in the Bay. Though numbers have fallen substantially in recent years, the Bay's commercial crab harvest has regularly exceeded 50 million pounds per year during the last two decades.[6] With the dockside price of crabs around $1 per pound for hard crabs and nearly $4 per pound for soft crabs, annual crab harvests have grossed more than $50 million over the last decade.

The dockside value of the crabbing industry represents only one part of the total revenue derived from the blue crab. There are forty-four crabmeat-processing plants around the Bay that employ over twelve hundred workers and have annual sales in excess of $30 million.[7] There are also truck drivers, bait suppliers, seafood dealers, restaurants, grocery stores, and gear providers that directly benefit from the crab harvest, as well as local hotels, fishing boat manufacturers, and mechanics that indirectly benefit from the resource. It has been estimated that the crab industry provides roughly $156 million a year in revenue to the region, revenue that is concentrated in many of the most isolated and least developed areas of Maryland and Virginia.[8]

THE BLUE CRAB (*CALLINECTES SAPIDUS*)

Callinectes sapidus, the blue-claw crab, or more commonly referred to simply as the blue crab, is a fascinating creature.[9] Throughout the course of its life, it undergoes three metamorphoses, molting dozens of times in the process, literally reinventing itself with each transformation. The blue crab starts life in its first larval stage, called zoea, as a minute organism that under a microscope looks more like a science fiction creature than a crab. Zoea are carried by currents to the Atlantic Ocean, molting roughly a half-dozen times, before returning to the seagrass beds where they were spawned. Upon returning to the Bay, they transform into their postlarval form called megalops. At this stage, they are still barely visible and take on the appearance of minuscule lobsters. With time, the creatures undergo a final transformation and take on the shape of tiny crabs, about one-fifth of an inch in size. Crabs undergo a series of molts before reaching their adult size of about five to seven inches (see figure 5.1).

Adult blue crabs differ substantially by gender and age. Females have what many watermen refer to as "painted fingers" because of their red-tipped claws.[10] The males lack this coloration and have characteristically blue claws. Immature female crabs, commonly referred to as "she-crabs," have V-shaped underbellies; and mature females, called "sooks," have U-shaped underbellies. The male crab, or "Jimmy," is often considerably larger than a female of the same age and prefers the less salty waters of the northern Chesapeake, while the females prefer the higher salinity levels closer to the Atlantic. The size difference between male and female crabs occurs because male crabs continue to molt and grow their entire lives and female crabs stop molting upon reaching maturity. As a consequence, crabs that are harvested from the lower Chesapeake, where females are more prevalent, tend to be smaller than crabs harvested in the upper reaches of the Chesapeake, where males are more abundant.

The blue crab expresses its legendary tenacity in a number of ways. As an opportunistic predator, blue crabs feed on a wide variety of available foods, including fish, plants, bivalves, and other blue crabs, especially when alternative food sources are scarce. They are fast, powerful creatures that have scarred the fingers of many a waterman and recreational fisherman. Even an immature crab that grabs hold on an exposed hand can easily puncture the skin and cause a great deal of pain.

The crab's mating practices also give insights into its brutish personality. As a female approaches her pubertal molt, a male crab grasps onto the immature female and carries her until she is ready to molt, fighting off rival males in the meantime. After mating, the male crab continues to grasp the female in a postcopulatory embrace that can last for several days. During this time, the male assures that no other crabs

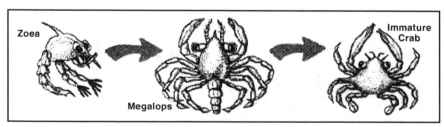

Figure 5.1.   Life Stages of the Blue Crab
Source: **Chesapeake Bay Program (2002a).**

eat his mate or attempt to fertilize her eggs. After the female's new shell hardens, marking the end of the mating process, the crabs go their separate ways, the female never to mate again.

One reason the species has proved to be so resilient to fishing pressure over the years is that female crabs can produce as many as eight million eggs in a single spawn. And since female crabs can store sperm from their mating encounter for more than two years and spawn multiple times during this period, a female may produce several million fertilized eggs throughout her life. Though only a small fraction of the larvae is likely to survive to maturity (many are eaten by predators and others fall victim to unsuitable water conditions), the reproductive prowess of the female crab adds to the species' resilience.

Another factor that has contributed to the crab's heartiness is its ability to survive in areas that are inhospitable to other species, including polluted water and water with low oxygen levels. While crabs are not immune to anoxic (no oxygen) and hypoxic (low oxygen) water conditions, they can tolerate oxygen levels that would be fatal to most Bay species. The Chesapeake Bay Program reports that crabs can survive in water with oxygen levels as low as 0.5 mg/L for as long as 4 hours, and most crabs can live in water with dissolved oxygen of only 3.0 mg/L indefinitely.[11]

To the amazement of many, the blue crab has even been able to tolerate some of the Bay's most polluted bodies of water, such as the Elizabeth River (Norfolk) and the Patapsco River (Baltimore). It was once feared that crabs that live in polluted waters might be particularly susceptible to toxic bioaccumulation because they tend to feed on bottom-dwelling animals and winter in sediments where it is likely that they are exposed to toxic conditions. But scientists have found that the animal's relatively short lifespan, usually only about three years, and its migratory patterns help to protect the blue crab from the long-term effects of toxic exposure.[12]

All told, the blue crab is one of the world's great survivors, with a fossil record dating back over a million years.[13] It is a hearty creature that is ideally suited for the Chesapeake Bay's shallow, brackish waters. The blue crab is an ecological treasure worthy of protection.

THE DECLINE OF THE BLUE CRAB

Given the natural fecundity, tenacity, and resilience of the blue crab, its declining numbers over the last decade have been a major cause of concern for those working to restore the Bay. If not the hearty blue crab, what species will be able to endure in the Chesapeake in future years? The fear is driven by the collapse of many of the Bay's once thriving fisheries. The oyster industry dominated commercial fishing in the region for a hundred years before overharvesting and disease caused the oyster population to fail. Other fisheries, such as that of the shad and Atlantic sturgeon, also once played important roles in the fishing industry before being virtually wiped out in the Bay. And even the striped bass, the Bay's success story, required a Baywide moratorium before experiencing an appreciable improvement in the late 1990s. Were the crab population to fail, it would put an end to the Bay's last major fishery, an end to a way of life that has flourished in watermen communities for over a hundred years, and, most likely, it would mark the symbolic end of the larger fight to save the Bay.

Figure 5.2 shows that in recent years commercial fishermen have used more gear to catch fewer crabs than at any other time in history. The line graph shows that the amount of gear used to catch crabs has steadily increased, rising to over 600,000 units of gear, five times greater than the amount that was used in the mid-1940s. The commercial harvest, on the other hand, has declined to less than 50 million pounds per year, or less than half the size of the 1993 harvest. Perhaps the most disturbing finding is that the trend shows no sign of reversing itself. If anything, the numbers suggest that the rate of decline has accelerated in recent years.[14]

There are several factors that have contributed to the decline of the blue crab in the Chesapeake Bay. The most obvious, and perhaps most important, factor is fishing pressure. In recent years, the fishery mortality rate has reached $F = .90$, which means that each year fishing pressure typically removes 90 percent of the blue crab's spawning potential.[15] In other words, 90 percent of the crabs that could have spawned were harvested by fishermen. While the impressive reproductive abilities of the crab have allowed this level of exploitation to continue without a collapse, scientists now believe that an F score of .7 (70 percent) should be the long-term target for a sustainable crab population.[16]

While fishing has undoubtedly taken its toll on the blue crab, it is by no means the only cause of the crab's relatively poor condition in the Chesapeake. Poor water quality has also played a major role in the decline of the blue crab. As discussed earlier, nutrient loads cause massive

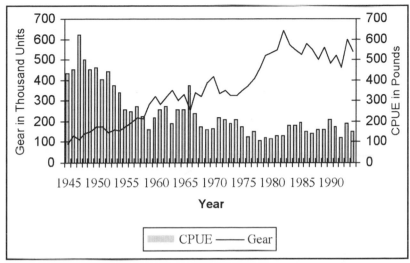

Figure 5.2. Fishing Effort and Catch per Unit Effort (CPUE) Chesapeake Bay Blue Crab Fishery
Source: **Chesapeake Bay Program (1997a, 39).**

algae blooms to occur in the Bay each summer, depleting water of its dissolved oxygen. At the height of summer, when the oxygen needs of the crab are the highest, due to their increased activity during this period, large areas of the Bay experience anoxic and hypoxic conditions that are unsuitable for supporting crabs. At the lower levels of the water column, where crabs live, the problem of low oxygen levels is particularly common.[17]

Poor water quality also affects the crab by adversely impacting its habitat, most importantly, aquatic grasses. Sediment and nutrient loads cloud much of the Bay's water, blocking out light and reducing the ability of underwater grasses to survive. The Bay's grasses, currently estimated at one-tenth their historic levels, assist crabs at various stages of their development. For example, grasses serve as natural nurseries for young crabs as they develop, providing postlarval and juvenile crabs with shelter from predators and a food-rich environment. One study found that juvenile crab density was thirty times greater in areas that had underwater grasses when compared to similar areas that did not contain grasses.[18]

Crabs in stressed populations are particularly susceptible to disease, putting the stock at further risk. Several studies have linked disease and stress in the blue crab.[19] Crab diseases can cause unsightly lesions on the crab's shell, blacken muscle tissue, reduce reproductive abilities, and even cause mortality. Many of the diseases are contagious to other crabs and can spread throughout a weakened population. Crabs are also susceptible to parasites, such as *Hematodinium perezi,* which have been identified in the lower Bay since 1994 and have been linked to crab mortality.[20] While crab diseases and parasites have not been a major cause of mortality for crabs in the past, the risk undoubtedly increases as the population comes under increased stress.

The blue crab population has not yet collapsed in the Chesapeake Bay, but more and more people within the scientific community feel the population is weakened to the point that any number of naturally occurring disturbances, such as floods or hurricanes, which periodically occur in the region, would be sufficient to trigger a collapse. Natural conditions are known to have a tremendous influence on the crab population, causing peaks and valleys in the population. The fear is that it is only a matter of time before a natural circumstance, combined with a weakened population, will devastate the Bay's blue crab population. A recent report by the National Oceanic and Atmospheric Administration (2001) warns:

> The consensus among technical committee members is that it is risky to remain in the current situation. When a weak year class arrives, there will be those that attribute the stock decline or collapse to unusual environmental conditions instead of fishing, but unusual environmental conditions are only unusual in the short term. Fishing mortality rate must be reduced and stock abundance should be increased as rapidly as possible. (3)

The experts agree that the blue crab population is fully exploited and near the point of collapse. They have called for immediate action to strengthen the crab stock before a natural disturbance pushes the crab population beyond a point from which it can naturally rebound.

THE BASIC MANAGEMENT NEEDS OF THE BLUE CRAB

The management needs of the Bay's blue crab have not fundamentally changed since the Chesapeake Bay Commission first called for more active management of the fishery in the early 1980s. At the forefront of the effort to protect the species is the push to reduce and control fishing efforts. In recent years, an increase in the amount of fishing gear used by commercial watermen, as well as growing pressure from recreational crabbers, has taken its toll on the crab. A consistent theme echoed in management plans and scientific recommendations for over a decade has been the call to decrease the annual harvest to a lower, more sustainable level.

There are several methods for limiting the commercial and recreational harvest of the blue crab. Traditional approaches taken by resource managers include reducing the length of the crabbing season, banning the use of crab dredges that allow watermen to harvest crabs during the winter months when they lay dormant, limiting the number of days or the number of hours that watermen can work, creating sanctuaries where crab harvesting is not permitted, limiting the number of commercial and/or recreational licenses issued, and creating limits to the number of crabs that each license holder can legally harvest each day. Other methods include creating a quota system that restricts the number of crabs a waterman harvests each season, but that allows fishermen to sell or purchase quotas according to their needs. Less-explored approaches include buying back fishing vessels or commercial fishing licenses from watermen and providing watermen with temporary subsidies or tax breaks to help offset the cost of limiting their catch. These approaches, while expensive, could help to correct short-term harvest pressures while preserving the economic vitality of communities that rely on income from the Bay.

Beyond the problems associated with overharvesting, resource managers and the scientific community have long warned against the deleterious effects of wasteful harvesting practices. Wasteful harvesting practices include taking small crabs that are of little commercial value and have not yet matured to breeding age, the harvesting of egg-bearing female crabs before they have the chance to release their eggs, and the use of poorly designed crab pots (i.e., crab traps). A 1990 study estimated that between 10 and 30 percent of crab pots are lost each year, either abandoned after the season or lost to storms or mismanagement.[21] These lost pots, or ghost pots, are made from galvanized mesh that is slow to erode and that can last for several seasons. Crabs that enter the ghost pots eventually die and attract additional crabs in a process commonly referred to as self-baiting that is responsible for the loss of untold numbers of crabs each year.

Solutions to wasteful harvesting practices include the use of cull rings that enable small crabs to escape crab pots without harm, banning the harvest of sponge crabs (i.e., egg-bearing crabs), and requiring the use of biodegradable escape hatches that guard against the dangers of ghost pots. A standard identification system for crab pots also helps to reduce the impact of ghost pots and improves accountability among watermen. Such a system enables natural resource law enforcement officers to better monitor pots, guard against unlicensed pots, and issue fines to watermen who fail to recover a certain percentage of their traps, creating a financial incentive for watermen to vigilantly manage their gear.

It is widely accepted within the scientific community that no long-term management plan for the blue crab can ignore the Bay's poor water quality. While it is true that the crab can survive for extended periods of time in water conditions that would kill many of the Bay's other aquatic species, the aquatic grasses that provide valuable habitat for the crab during vulnerable periods in its life cycle have proved far less resistant to poor water quality than the crab. The widespread loss of underwater grasses in the Bay should be corrected to help secure the future of the blue crab.

The primary method for addressing the Bay's poor water quality, discussed in detail in previous chapters, is to limit the amount of nutrients and sediments that enter the Bay from point and nonpoint sources. Secondary steps to help restore underwater grasses include replanting grasses in areas where they once flourished and controlling exotic species that consume grasses. For example, the mute swan, a beautiful but destructive species that feeds on aquatic grasses was introduced to North America in the nineteenth century and is now common throughout the Chesapeake Bay. With over seven thousand birds reported in the Bay, these large animals, weighing up to twenty-five pounds, graze on wide areas of underwater grasses, damaging an already endangered natural resource.[22]

The final management need of the crab, and perhaps the most difficult to achieve, is for resource managers in Virginia and Maryland to adopt a truly coordinated management approach. The blue crab recognizes no political boundaries and typically travels between Virginia and Maryland waters throughout its life cycle, making it an interstate resource. Inadequate management in one state inevitably affects the crab fishery in the other state. Likewise, adopting strict regulations in one state delivers unintended advantages to economic rivals in the other state. Only through a coordinated effort can this management dilemma be overcome. Bistate coordination enables resource managers to divide the burden of crabbing restrictions in an equitable manner and to pursue a unified strategy that reflects the crab's Baywide presence, helping to reduce the need for more aggressive restrictions in the future.

There are several options for pursuing a Baywide management approach. At one end of the management spectrum is a bistate advisory committee that recommends Baywide regulatory action. This is exactly what was created in 1996 when the Chesapeake Bay Commission created the Bi-State Blue Crab Advisory Committee (BBCAC). This committee brings together many of the region's leading marine scientists, resource managers, economists, environmental advocates, and commercial crabbers. BBCAC engages in extensive analysis and often heated debates regarding the health of the crab stock and management options. It was this committee that recommended the 15 percent reduction in harvest pressures that has guided regulatory actions in Virginia and Maryland since 2001. This approach to Baywide resource management provides essential dialogue between the states, but lacks regulatory authority and enforcement power.

At the other end of the management spectrum would be a bistate regulatory board that goes beyond BBCAC's advisory role and promulgates enforceable management regulations for the Bay. Supporters of this approach hold that a bistate regulatory agency would be better situated to overcome the competitive forces that can obstruct regulatory action at the state and local levels. In other words, a bistate agency could promulgate regulations across the Bay, improving the chance that neither state gains an unfair commercial advantage and that regulations are enacted based on the ecological needs of the blue crab. Such a regulatory body is not without precedent in the area. The Potomac River Fisheries Commission has operated as a semiautonomous regulatory body for the Potomac River since 1959. This commission was created to establish management regulations for the disputed Potomac River, which runs between the two states but which is generally considered to fall within Maryland's jurisdiction.[23] The commission establishes fishing guidelines for the entire Potomac River, and the fishery agencies of Virginia and Maryland provide law enforcement. The commission was created to achieve a coordinated management approach for Virginia and Maryland's shared river. In a similar fashion, a regulatory commission could be created to manage Virginia and Maryland's shared interest in the living resources of the Bay, though such an approach has never been attempted.

FACTORS COMPLICATING BLUE CRAB
MANAGEMENT FOR THE CHESAPEAKE BAY

While the management needs of the crab are fairly straightforward—that is, leave enough crabs to assure the population can successfully replenish itself each year, minimize wasteful crabbing practices, and protect the crab's habitat—several factors have complicated management efforts. One such factor is the cyclical nature of the crab stock. Watermen and researchers have long been aware that a poor year for crabs might be followed by a record harvest the following year. These fluctuations have led many observers, watermen in particular, to question the need for restrictive regulations. Moreover, the cyclical nature of the stock has fostered scientific debate regarding the precise size of the reproductive stock that needs to be preserved from year to year. Together, the watermen's confidence that the population will rebound and the scientific community's uncertainty regarding sustainable levels have helped to foster a climate that promotes inaction.

An often-overlooked factor that also complicates coordinated management and planning is the fluctuation in harvests across regions and among harvest types (i.e., the hard-shell and soft-shell harvests). Crab populations can differ substantially across the Bay depending on habitat conditions in a particular area and relative fishing pressures. A recent report by the Bi-State Blue Crab Advisory Committee shows that while harvests of hard crabs have generally declined across the Bay, the numbers have fallen the most in areas such as Maryland's lower eastern section of the Bay and Virginia's upper western region, where hard crab harvests fell by 50 percent between 1997 and 2001.[24] Soft crab harvests have generally declined less across the Bay and have remained fairly stable in the heavily fished areas of the Tangier/Pocomoke Sounds. These regional differences have the ability to color one's perspective on the health of the Bay's blue crab population, causing some to favor more restrictive measures, while others see less of a need for restrictive regulatory action.

But the factor that poses the greatest challenge to management efforts is the migratory patterns of the crab. Male crabs, which molt throughout their lives and grow much larger than female crabs, prefer the low-salinity waters of Maryland's northern Bay. Female crabs, which stop molting after they breed and are generally smaller than males, prefer the high-salinity waters of Virginia's southern Bay. This single biological fact has led to countless management debates between Virginia and Maryland resource managers. Regulations that restrict or ban harvesting egg-bearing crabs disproportionately affect Virginia watermen because a larger portion of their harvest is comprised of sponge crabs. Likewise, restrictions that increase minimum size limits are also felt the hardest by Virginia watermen, since female crabs that prefer Virginia waters tend to be smaller than males that prefer the less salty waters to the north.

This difference has fueled a management debate that has worked to stifle coordinated management efforts in the Bay. Maryland watermen accuse the wasteful practices of Virginia watermen for the decline in the Bay's crab population, citing Virginia's more liberal crab regulations that permit Virginia watermen to harvest egg-bearing females, smaller crabs, and to dredge for crabs in the winter. Virginia watermen claim that imposing Maryland-style restrictions on Virginia watermen would be unfair and disastrous for Virginia's struggling crab industry. Overcoming this impasse remains one of the most important steps toward achieving a sensible management policy for the Bay's blue crab.

THE STRUGGLE FOR A SENSIBLE MANAGEMENT STRATEGY

Laws regulating the Bay's blue crab harvest date back to the early twentieth century when Virginia, in 1916, and Maryland, in 1917, outlawed harvesting undersized crabs. For much of the twentieth century, size restrictions were sufficient to sustain this remarkably resilient species. With fishing pressures increasing during the 1980s and 1990s and water conditions remaining in a poor state, it became apparent that the traditional hands-off approach would no longer be sufficient for managing the crab.

The decline in the Bay's other major fisheries had a mixed impact on the blue crab. On one hand, the collapse of other species led to a substantial increase in commercial fishing pressure placed on the crab, due to the lack of alternative fisheries in the Bay. With oysters and many finfish at record lows, watermen increasingly looked to the profitable blue crab harvest to support the Bay's once diverse commercial fishing industry. On the other hand, the collapse of the Bay's primary fisheries helped bring attention to the failure of existing resource management efforts and helped to fuel the push for a Baywide management strategy for the blue crab.

Even with widespread attention given to the decline in the Bay's major fisheries, the fight to achieve a sensible, Baywide management strategy for the protection of the long-term health of the crab has proved exceedingly difficult. Calls by the Chesapeake Bay Commission in the early 1980s for Virginia and Maryland to adopt a unified management strategy for the Bay's living resources went unheeded. Scientists, resource managers, and ecologists continued to disagree over the basic management needs of the crab, while commercial and recreational crabbers insisted that the crab stock was healthy and that additional regulations were unnecessary. A Bi-State Fisheries Advisory Working Group was formed in 1984 only to be disbanded in 1986 when Virginia and Maryland representatives could not overcome their management differences. It took nearly a decade of prodding by the Chesapeake Bay Commission and the failure of many of the Bay's major fisheries for the Chesapeake Bay Program to complete the Bay's first unified fishery management plan (FMP) in 1989.

The political struggle to adopt a unified management strategy did not end with the Bay Program's 1989 management plan. Since the Bay Program lacks regulatory power, it was up to the states to consider the five problem areas identified by the Bay Program plan and to pursue strategies for addressing the problems, something the states have been slow to accomplish.[25] It was not until the mid-1990s, when declining harvests and rising prices brought attention to the blue crab's poor condition, that the states began to take serious steps toward addressing the management needs of the crab.

By the mid-1990s, Maryland and Virginia limited the number of commercial licenses issued, making commercial crabbing in the states a limited-access fishery. Virginia created seasonal sanctuaries where crabbing was prohibited, issued recreational fishing licenses, imposed gear restrictions, enforced a crabbing season, and improved its cull ring requirements. Maryland passed emergency regulations in 1995 that moved regulations beyond the state's existing ban on sponge crabs and gear and size restrictions. The emergency measures shortened the season, limited the workday, and prohibited crabbing one day per week. These initial steps proved insufficient to bring about the desired widespread improvement for the blue crab, and harvests failed to rebound. By the mid-1990s, it was more apparent than ever that a coordinated effort was required to successfully manage the crab.

As mentioned earlier, coordinated management took a major step forward in 1996 when the Chesapeake Bay Commission created the Bi-

State Blue Crab Advisory Committee (BBCAC). Unlike the advisory committee that had failed a decade earlier, the new committee has successfully provided a forum for representatives from the two states to discuss the management problems facing the crab. The committee, which receives funding from both states, has completed several studies of the industry and has issued suggestions for protecting the blue crab stock. In 2001, with crab numbers near historic lows, BBCAC recommended a 15 percent reduction in fishing pressure to be phased in over three years to help restore the Bay's crab stock.[26] The major difference between the BBCAC's recommendations and the recommendations issued in the Bay Program's fishery plans in 1989 and 1997 was that the BBCAC specified a harvest reduction goal for the entire Bay, something that had never before been attempted.

Since BBCAC issued its recommendations, both states have agreed in principle to the 15 percent reduction target. Nonetheless, the larger objective of achieving coordinated management that maximizes the benefit of regulations remains an elusive goal. The states are free to enact their own reduction plans and to modify them as they see fit. As a consequence, there remain stark differences between the regulatory approaches adopted by Maryland and Virginia. Rather than pursuing a unified approach that could promote complementary actions between the states and increase the overall effectiveness of regulations, the states continue along separate management courses. (See table 5.1 for a comparison of management practices of the two states.)

Comparing the regulations on sponge crabs (egg-bearing female crabs) provides insights into the opportunities that are lost due to uncoordinated management. Officials in Maryland and Virginia have long realized the negative consequences of harvesting sponge crabs. Removing a sponge crab does more than remove a single crab from the stock; it also removes millions of eggs and disproportionately influences the reproductive abilities of the population. With this in mind, Maryland bolstered its ban on sponge crabs in 2002 by making it illegal not only to catch sponge crabs, but also to possess them. This ban made it illegal for sponge crabs that are legally caught in Virginia to be processed in Maryland. The rule was enacted in an attempt to close Maryland's market to Virginia's sponge crab harvest.

Without cooperation from Virginia, however, the possession ban has had several unintended consequences. First, the ban hurts Maryland's thirty crab-picking houses. Since sponge crabs are more abundant

Table 5.1.   Major Differences in Commercial Crabbing Regulations in Virginia and Maryland (2002)

	Virginia	Maryland
Limited Access:		
Season	April 1–November 30	April 1–December 15
	December 1–March 31 (dredge)	No winter dredge
Gear Restrictions:		
Hard Crab Pots	500 per licensee	300 per licensee
	No limit per vessel	900 per vessel (max)
Size Restrictions:		
Male crabs	5 inches	5¼ inches
Egg-Bearing Females	Permitted (except in late stages)	Possession ban
Immature Females	5 inches	5¼ inches
Peeler crabs	3 inches	3½ inches
Soft Shells	3½ inches	4 inches
Daily Catch Restrictions:		
Dredge Limits	17 barrels per vessel (12/1–3/31)	None
Pots	17 barrels per vessel (4/1–5/31)	None
Spatial Restrictions:		
Sanctuaries	Deep-water sanctuaries (6/1–9/15)	Some
	(927 square miles)	Restricted Areas

earlier in the season than hard crabs, Maryland processors had previously relied on Virginia's early sponge crab harvest to support the industry until Maryland's hard crab harvest peaked later in the summer. With the possession ban in place, Maryland processors have lost business while Virginia processors reap the rewards of Virginia's lenient sponge crab policies. The increased supply of sponge crabs arriving at Virginia processing plants also works to drive down crab prices in the state, creating incentives for Virginia crabbers to increase fishing pressure to account for diminishing returns. Likewise, the price of crabmeat in Maryland, because of its limited supply, becomes less competitive than the price of crabmeat processed in Virginia, where supply is high. And since the ban does not extend to processed crabmeat, only to the crabs, the ban actually increases the chance that crabmeat eaten in Maryland comes from egg-bearing crabs caught and processed in Virginia.

The example illustrates how the good intentions of policymakers in one state can be frustrated by the lack of interstate coordination. The Maryland policymakers hoped to influence the behavior of watermen in

Virginia by limiting the market for their sponge crabs. Lacking the ability to meaningfully influence Virginia's regulatory policies, Maryland enacted restrictions that hurt its crab processors and that are unlikely to deliver the intended environmental outcomes. Had a bistate regulatory body been in place, a more effective approach could have been taken that spread the burden of crab reductions more equitably between the two states, while at the same time taking into account the negative impact of the sponge crab harvest.

The sponge crab example is not unique. Regulatory measures in one management area inevitably carry unintended consequences that are exacerbated by the lack of Baywide coordination. For example, closing the season early in one state inevitably provides benefits to crabbers in the other state. It is not only that crabbers in a state with a longer season can harvest more crabs; they can also receive more return for their effort, since they sell their crabmeat into a limited market. Likewise, uneven size restrictions and allowing winter dredging in one state and not the other can also lead to unintended economic benefits to the less restrictive state.

CONCLUSION

More than a decade after the Bay Program issued its first management plan for the blue crab and two decades after the Chesapeake Bay Commission began calling for a coordinated management strategy, the states continue to struggle with disjointed management approaches that reflect political boundaries more than the ecological needs of the crab. Though steps have been taken to coordinate blue crab management goals, fishery management remains a largely uncoordinated and reactionary activity in the Chesapeake Bay. With the collapse of the oyster and other Bay fisheries, many were hopeful that resource managers from Virginia and Maryland would be able to overcome their differences and adopt a unified approach for managing the Bay's last major fishery. Unfortunately, proactive, coordinated management has proved to be an elusive goal, and the long-term future of the blue crab remains uncertain.

Ultimately, it is the political process that must take responsibility for the current state of the crab. It is the political process that promulgates rules regarding resource management and it is the political process that has failed to adequately protect the blue crab population from the brink of collapse. The political forces that have transformed the long-term interests of watermen, the desires of the environmental community, the advice of the research community, and the good intentions of policymakers into a regulatory record that is littered with suboptimum rules forms the focus of the next chapter.

6

Battling over the Blue Crab

The Politics of Crab Management
in Virginia and Maryland

If Maryland destroys the young female crab, then we are sure that she will not reach Virginia to hatch out her young. On the other hand, if the Commonwealth of Virginia permits the mother crab to be taken by winter dredging near the Capes, or the female with the bunion of eggs, this great industry is surely doomed in the Chesapeake Bay.

> —Conservation Department of Maryland (1923), *The First Annual Report of the Conservation Department of the State of Maryland*

You have to realize that if you get between a waterman and a crab, it is like getting between a grizzly bear and a piece of meat—they are going to run over you. That does not mean you do not preserve grizzly bears.

> —Tom Horton (2002a), columnist and author

On the evening of September 8, 1924, Maryland Governor Albert C. Ritchie left Annapolis harbor aboard the state's steamer for what was billed as a historic meeting with Virginia's Governor R. Lee Trinkle. The talks were scheduled to take place the following day on the Potomac River aboard the *Commodore Maury*, Virginia's police steamer. It was a much-anticipated meeting marking the first time that the governors and fishery commissioners from the two states were to come together to discuss options for addressing Baywide crab management.

As the officials departed for the meeting, a storm swept across the Bay from the southeast producing uncharacteristically rough seas and forcing the Maryland delegation to take safe harbor on the Patuxent

River. The following day when Governor Ritchie and his entourage arrived at the designated meeting spot, the Virginia group and their boat were nowhere to be found. The *Commodore Maury* arrived several hours later without Governor Trinkle, who had fallen during the storm the night before and broken his arm, causing the ill-fated meeting to be canceled and putting off the first attempt at bistate blue crab management for another day.[1]

The historic gubernatorial conference did eventually take place two months later on solid ground in Annapolis, Maryland. At this meeting Maryland's Conservation Commissioner Swepson Earle and Governor Ritchie made the now common argument that Virginia's practice of harvesting egg-bearing female crabs, outlawed in Maryland since 1916, and Virginia's winter dredging season were driving down the Bay's crab population. Following the meeting, Commissioner Earle issued the ominous warning, "This great industry may yet be saved for the watermen of both states, but the General Assembly of the Commonwealth of Virginia must act in 1926 or it will be too late."[2] Earle's predictions, though premature, clearly delineated the management differences that had evolved between the two states, as well as the interdependency of the fishery.

Today, Virginia continues to allow the harvesting of egg-bearing crabs and a winter dredge season, while both practices have long been banned in Maryland. As the crab population has fallen in recent years and the once great industry that Earle referred to struggles to survive, Maryland and Virginia have yet to implement a Baywide management approach for the blue crab. Competition for the increasingly limited resource, not cooperation and collaboration, continues to define blue crab management between the two states.

The history, structure, and composition of a regulatory body can greatly influence the regulations that it promulgates. With the responsibility for managing the Bay's natural resources divided between Virginia and Maryland, rather than resting in a single Baywide regulatory body, it is necessary to explore the characteristics of the regulatory agencies of both states to understand the political context in which management policies are promulgated for the Bay. The distinct regulatory strategies that have emerged between the states reflect not only the dissimilar nature of the crab fishery in Maryland and Virginia, but also the distinct characteristics of their regulatory bodies.

BLUE CRAB MANAGEMENT IN VIRGINIA

The Commonwealth of Virginia boasts an extensive history of marine resource management. The state's first resource management agency, the Virginia Fish Commission, the predecessor to the modern Virginia Marine Resources Commission (VMRC), was established in 1875. It was created to help protect the state's fisheries, most importantly, the oyster fishery that dominated commercial fishing in the state for much of the nineteenth and twentieth centuries.[3] Originally, the agency functioned as an advisory board that recommended management legislation to the state's General Assembly, in a similar manner to the way the Bi-State Blue Crab Advisory Committee currently advises the states of Maryland and Virginia.

In 1897, control of the Virginia Oyster Navy—established to help protect Virginia oyster beds from the growing problem of oyster pirates—was transferred to the Fish Commission, giving the commission enforcement powers it had previously lacked.[4] Later, law enforcement would be transferred to locally controlled marine patrols that receive funding from the Virginia Marine Resources Commission. By 1920, the agency, now named the State Fisheries Commission, took control of oyster administration and centrally administered shellfish bed leasing. In 1968, the commission was renamed the Marine Resources Commission to reflect its broadening responsibilities and the Bay's growing environmental problems. Regulatory authority continued to reside firmly within the General Assembly until the mid-1980s, when the state's Fishery Management Act of 1984 was passed, transferring many regulatory powers from the legislature to the Marine Resources Commission. By the end of the 1980s, the state's Marine Resources Commission possessed sufficient regulatory authority to make it a powerful management force.

It is important to note that Virginia's Marine Resources Commission evolved from a fisheries commission that was created to protect and enhance the state's commercial fishing industry, not to pursue broad ecological objectives.[5] To this day, the commission remains an industry-centered body, with close ties to the state's commercial fishing industry. The legacy of these relationships can be seen most clearly in the composition of the nine-member Marine Resources Commission.[6] William Pruitt has chaired the commission since 1983. Pruitt is a native Virginian, born on Tangier Island in the heart of the Bay's crabbing industry, where both his father and grandfather made their living as commercial watermen. Commissioner Chadwick Ballard's family owns and operates Ballard Fish and Oyster Company and Cherrystone Aqua-Farms. Commissioner S. Lake Cowart Jr., whose family owns Cowart Seafood Corporation, joined the commission in 1996, taking a position formerly occupied by his father from 1980 to1988. Also on the commission are Kenneth Wayne Williams, a commercial waterman for more than thirty years, and F. Wayne McLeskey, a multimillionaire real estate developer and owner of the largest marina in Virginia. McLeskey serves as the commission's recreational fishing representative. The commission also includes John W. White and Henry Lane Hull. White is an Eastern Shore native, while Hull lives in Northumberland County, a rural area heavily influenced by the commercial watermen of Virginia's Western Shore. Completing the commission are representatives Laura Belle Gordy, whose son is a waterman, and Gordon Birkett, a former marina owner and lifelong recreational fisherman.[7]

It is a citizens' commission that is heavily influenced by the interests of watermen and recreational crabbers, rather than conservationists and scientists. In fact, requirements governing the composition of the commission call for a commercial waterman to fill at least one of the positions and a licensed recreational fisherman to fill another position. Absent from the commission are marine scientists, economists, representatives from environmental organizations, and representatives from nonfishing areas—though representatives from these areas have the opportunity to testify before the commission at its many public hearings.

While the composition of the commission makes it an easy target for environmental groups and critics of the commission's management policies, the regulatory body is not without its management accomplishments. In particular, during the last decade, as evidence regarding the crab's decline continued to mount and public concern translated into public pressure, the commission enacted significant protective measures, some of which were strongly opposed by watermen and recreational crabbers. The commission implemented licensing requirements, crabbing seasons, gear restrictions, and daily time restrictions, among other regulations. In fact, Virginia has been a leader in requiring recreational crabbing licenses and creating crab sanctuaries. The regulatory record of the commission over the last decade suggests that when presented with overwhelming scientific evidence and substantial public pressure, the commission is capable of making difficult management decisions.

Nonetheless, its recent management accomplishments have done little to quell persistent criticism of the commission. In particular, the commission has been strongly criticized for continuing to allow the state's controversial winter dredge season and sponge crab harvest. The commission's detractors are quick to note that the commission's regulatory actions have been slow to develop and have consistently fallen short of the actions taken by the state's neighbor to the north.

BLUE CRAB MANAGEMENT IN MARYLAND

Maryland, like Virginia, also boasts a lengthy tradition of natural resource management. Maryland passed its first laws protecting game and fish in 1654, more than a hundred years before the nation declared its independence and just twenty years after Maryland was settled. One interesting example of early wildlife management in Maryland was the creation of bounties on natural predators, such as wolves, which competed with early settlers for fish and fowl. The idea behind such bounties was that by reducing the number of predators, game in the region would be more plentiful and livestock would be safer.[8] Though hardly an example of modern resource management practices, the early bounties do suggest that settlers in the area have long been aware of the limited nature of the watershed's natural resources and the role that humans can play in protecting nature's bounty.

By 1868, Maryland had its own oyster police, and in 1896 the state established its first state game warden. As was the case in Virginia, the agency in charge of marine resource management changed names several times as its responsibilities increased. The state game warden (1896–1922) was replaced by the Conservation Commission (1922–1935), which was replaced by the Conservation Department (1935–1939), which was replaced by the Department of Game and Inland Fish (1939–1941), which was replaced by the Board of Natural Resources/Department of Game and Inland Fish (1941–1969).[9]

Until the late 1960s, resource management in Maryland followed a pattern similar to that of Virginia. The day-to-day management of natural resources had increasingly been delegated from the state's legislative body, which in Maryland only meets ninety days per year, to the executive agencies that were headed by various commissions. In 1969, however, Maryland underwent a series of reforms that were initiated by its newly elected governor, Marvin Mandel. The reforms reflected Mandel's desire to strengthen the state's resource management practices and the general public's growing interest in environmental matters. Chief among the changes was the creation of the Department of Natural Resources, headed by a single cabinet-level secretary who reports directly to the governor.[10] The secretary of natural resources was given control over each of the state's resource management agencies, and the commissions that previously controlled resource management in the state were relegated to advisory roles. This move streamlined resource management in the state, created a direct line of responsibility to the governor, and wrested power away from the natural resource commissions.[11]

Today, the regulatory process in Maryland differs substantially from the commission-centered management structure that remains in place in Virginia. In Maryland, regulations are promulgated directly from the secretary of natural resources, often at the request of the governor and in consultation with the scientific community and the secretary's director of fisheries services.[12] As a gubernatorial appointment, the secretary of natural resources remains sensitive to the governor's environmental goals, giving the governor a great deal of influence over the agency.[13] After regulations have been crafted, they undergo a period of public comment and review at which time watermen and recreational fishermen, as well as the environmental community and the general public, are provided a forum to respond to regulatory proposals. Following this public review, the secretary of natural resources may choose to revise the regulations or may choose to send the regulation directly to the General Assembly. The General Assembly's oversight committee—the Administrative Executive Legislative Review Committee—then considers whether to support or reject the regulations. If regulations lack support from the General Assembly's review committee, as was the case with recent crab regulations, the governor has the authority to circumvent the legislative body and enact regulations without legislative action. However, if a sufficient portion of the General Assembly strongly opposes actions by the Department of Natural Resources and the governor, the assembly maintains the authority to strip away regulatory powers from the department or to enact alternative legislation that would supersede agency regulations, though these actions would most likely require sufficient support to override an executive veto and are rarely attempted.[14]

Given the secretary's central role in Maryland's regulatory process, it is interesting to compare the background of the person who currently occupies this position to the background of the people who comprise Virginia's Marine Resource Commission. As previously discussed, most of the members of Virginia's commission are directly or indirectly associated with the state's fishing or boating industries. The background of Maryland's chief marine resource manager is quite different. J. Charles "Chuck" Fox, Maryland's current secretary of natural resources, held three positions in the U.S. Environmental Protection Agency during the Clinton administration, including Assistant Administrator for Water, where he was responsible for the implementation of the Clean Water Act. He has also served as a consultant or board member for several environmental organizations including Friends of the Earth, the Environmental Policy Institute, the Sierra Club, and the Maryland League of Conservation Voters. Before his appointment to the Department of Natural Resources in August 2001, Fox was a senior policy adviser to the Chesapeake Bay Foundation, the area's leading environmental advocacy group.

Fox's professional background is indicative of the larger philosophic divide that has become apparent between marine resource management in Virginia and Maryland. Under the direction of environmental advocates like Chuck Fox and the state's other recent natural resource directors (Sarah Taylor-Rogers, John Griffin, and Torrey Brown), Maryland has come to stress natural resources, such as the blue crab, as ecological assets to be preserved for their intrinsic value, while management in Virginia continues to stress the economic and recreational value of such resources. This is not to say that resource managers in Maryland are not concerned with the commercial fishing industry and that managers in Virginia do not appreciate the ecological value of the resource. The difference is more subtle and mostly a matter of emphasis. Industry-centered resource management, as in Virginia's case, puts a premium on stakeholder involvement— that is, the involvement of commercial and recreational fishermen. Maryland's ecologically-centered management considers the economic impact of a regulation as one factor among many and gives no special place to industry interests in the regulatory process.

Though both states desire to protect the health of the crab, the different management structures and the broader philosophical differences can lead resource managers in different directions. At the most basic level, the difference helps to explain why Maryland's Department of Natural Resources has moved more aggressively than Virginia's regulators in recent years. Maryland was first to limit the workday of watermen, require a day off during the week for watermen, increase size requirements, and ban the possession of sponge crabs, all moves that were strongly opposed by industry forces. Virginia has been far more willing to invest in less proven management methods, such as the creation of deepwater crab sanctuaries that, while still opposed by watermen, are generally viewed as far less threatening to the industry than the types of regulations being pursued in Maryland.

ENVIRONMENTAL THEORY: TOWARD A DEEPER UNDERSTANDING OF BLUE CRAB MANAGEMENT

Differences in the regulatory structure and focus of the two states certainly complicate management of the Bay's blue crab. At the very least, divided management of this single natural resource makes the regulatory process unnecessarily complicated, providing numerous political barriers that must be overcome to achieve sensible Baywide management. However, the bureaucratic maze and the cross-state differences discussed previously represent only a small dimension of the political difficulties successful crab management faces. The remainder of this section explores the less obvious political forces that constrain natural resource management practices. The study's theoretical framework (see figure 6.1) is applied to blue crab management in the two states, show-

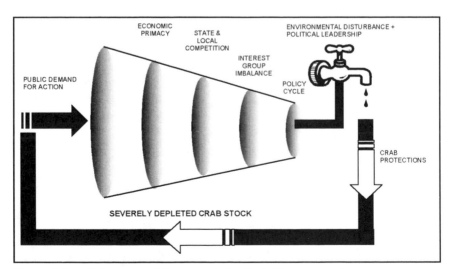

Figure 6.1. A Conceptual Framework for Crab Management
Graphic design by Christine Jamison.

ing how economic concerns, interest group politics, divided government, and the policy cycle affect resource management. This section further explains how more than a century of natural resource management
in the two states has failed to protect the blue crab from the brink of
collapse.

ECONOMIC PRIMACY AND BLUE CRAB
MANAGEMENT FOR THE CHESAPEAKE BAY

As discussed in chapter 5, the crabbing industry represents a substantial
economic force in the states of Virginia and Maryland, making crab regulations an important economic issue, as well as an ecological concern.
With roughly 50 percent of the country's crab harvest coming from the
Chesapeake Bay, the annual harvest regularly yields dockside values in
excess of $50 million a year.[15] Add to this the more than forty crabmeat-
processing plants, which employ over twelve hundred workers and have
annual sales in excess of $30 million, and the numerous local restau-
rants and fish markets that benefit from the Bay's annual harvest, and
one begins to appreciate the economic importance of this industry.[16]

Beyond the revenue generated from harvesting blue crabs, there
are several factors that magnify the economic significance of the industry and, in turn, the political weight given to crabbing interests. Chief
among these is the fact that the economic impact of crab regulations is
generally not evenly distributed, but disproportionately affects a small
number of areas that rely heavily on commercial fishing for revenue.
Such places as Tangier Island, Smith Island, and Crisfield offer few economic opportunities beyond commercial fishing, and as the Bay's other
fisheries have failed, these areas have become increasingly dependent on
the blue crab harvest. In such places as these, commercial crabbing is the
lifeblood of the local economy. Regulatory strategies that restrict the annual harvest and offer no financial relief to commercial watermen are
particularly hard felt and aggressively resisted in these areas.

Regulations can also disproportionately affect areas involved in
crabmeat processing. For example, in Dorchester County, Maryland,
home to twenty-one of the state's thirty crabmeat-processing plants,
regulations that have little impact elsewhere in the state can cause substantial impact on the local economy. A recent study by University of
Maryland researchers estimated that Maryland's new crab regulations,

which ban possession of sponge crabs and harvesting of male crabs less than 5¼ inches, will cost the state 539 jobs and $13.5 million in lost revenue.[17] The majority of the loss will come in Dorchester County, where the study predicts 349 jobs and $10.3 million in revenue will be lost as a consequence of the regulations. The disproportionate economic impact makes the issue a pressing concern for elected officials and industry leaders in the area, amplifying the political resistance to the regulations.

Another important factor to address when considering the economic resistance to crab regulations is the substantial cost associated with commercial crabbing. A commercial crabber's expenses include the price of a boat, gear, boat insurance, dock space, licenses, bait, fuel, and maintenance. A recent study by the Bi-State Blue Crab Advisory Committee estimated that the average daily cost for commercial crabbers in Virginia was $279 and in Maryland $228.[18] In order for the commercial crabbing industry to remain viable, these substantial expenses must be offset by a steady supply of crabs, a fact that often pits the short-term economic interests of the commercial crabber against the long-term interests of resource managers. It is not that crabbers are against taking protective action for the crab; after all, no group has as large a stake in the crab stock as commercial fishermen. It is that their short-term economic commitments often do not allow them the luxury of supporting costly regulations.

A final factor that augments the economic importance of the crab industry is its ability to provide relatively high-paying jobs to people with modest education levels and few comparable opportunities off the water. A recent survey by the Bi-State Blue Crab Advisory Committee found that among commercial crabbers in Virginia, 66 percent report having a high school degree or less as their highest level of formal education, with 32 percent reporting that they had not graduated from high school.[19] For Maryland's commercial crabbers, 64 percent reported no formal education beyond high school, with 20 percent lacking a high school degree. For many of these watermen, access to alternative professions, especially professions that offer the type of independence that commercial crabbers enjoy, is extremely limited.

Together, these economic factors help to give the crab industry more political capital than its revenues alone might warrant. The central question facing resource managers is how to successfully manage the crab population without putting undue hardship on the communities and watermen that rely on income from the annual crab harvest. In other words, how can the cost of protecting the crab be absorbed in a way that does not drive watermen out of business?

Standard regulatory approaches (e.g., closing the season early, mandating days off during the week, limiting the workday to eight hours, limiting the amount of gear used, and increasing minimum-size requirements) place the economic burden on watermen and, consequently, some of the region's poorest communities. Given the economic consequences of regulations like these, it is not surprising that political actors have been slow to pursue this course of action and have adopted these types of regulations only after overwhelming evidence suggested the crab population was on a dangerous decline.

More creative approaches that attempt to protect the crab *and* the communities that depend on the crabbing industry (e.g., gear and license buy-back programs, temporary subsidies to encourage harvest reductions, or price guarantees) transfer the cost of crab protection to the general public. These strategies also carry a hefty political cost. Under tight budgetary constraints, it is hard to imagine lawmakers dipping into public funds to subsidize an industry that is at least partially responsible for the Bay's decline. At the end of the day, the unwillingness to spread the economic burden of crab protection to the general public and the reluctance to impose painful restrictions on watermen has contributed to a regulatory climate that tends to obstruct proactive, long-term crab management practices.

INTEREST GROUP POLITICS AND
BLUE CRAB MANAGEMENT FOR THE BAY

Interest group representation in the arena of blue crab politics is far more complex than we saw for agriculture policy and more complex than Olson and other interest group scholars might have predicted. There is no equivalent to the farm bureau for watermen, neither nationally nor at the state level. In fact, interest group formation and maintenance for the crab industry, both for watermen and seafood processors, has proved to be a difficult task. Unlike the well-organized, politically savvy groups that represent agriculture, the crabbing industry tends to be represented by dozens of small and disconnected professional associations spread across the region. These organizations represent commercial watermen and processing plants, as well as recreational fishermen. What they have in common is a shared desire to maintain a steady supply of blue crabs. What divides them is intense competition for the Bay's limited crab stock.

By their very nature, watermen tend to be fiercely independent and pragmatic political actors, reluctant to join distant political organizations that pursue abstract objectives. This independent spirit contributes to the character of the seafood industry's various trade associations, which tend to be small independent groups dominated by parochial concerns. The associations often represent commercial fishing in a particular region of the Bay, such as the Lower Chesapeake Bay Watermen's Association, or a specific aspect of the larger seafood-processing industry, such as the Virginia Soft Crab Producers' Association.

Since a given regulation can adversely affect one aspect of the industry while at the same time providing benefits to other parts of the industry, crab interests rarely speak with a unified voice and have been unable to organize under a Baywide umbrella group. Maryland's recent ban on the possession of egg-bearing crabs provides a good example of how regulations can divide the industry, hurting crabmeat-processing plants in Maryland, while providing an economic boon to processing plants in Virginia. Likewise, recent regulations that increased minimum-size restrictions in Maryland have delivered unintended economic benefits to watermen in Virginia. There are similar conflicts of interest between commercial and recreational watermen, between crabbers who dredge and those who rely on pots, between crabbers who focus on peeler crabs and those who harvest hard crabs, and so on.

Beyond conflicts of interest that divide the groups, there are often heated disagreements over political strategies. For example, following the 2001 regulations that passed in Maryland, watermen in the state divided over the proper political response to the regulations. Larry Simns, head of the Maryland Watermen's Association, conceded the regulations were inevitable and chose a moderate strategy that stressed dialogue and cooperation with Maryland regulators, rather than pursuing a more aggressive approach. Outraged by the new regulations and feeling betrayed by the Maryland Watermen's Association, two splinter groups, the Blue Crab Conservation Coalition and the Chesapeake, Atlantic and Coastal Bay's Watermen's Coalition, opted for a more aggressive strategy. They chose legal action, which eventually failed, and chose to publicly criticize Simns and the state association that he heads. The conflict further divided Maryland's watermen and seafood processors, leaving feelings of animosity between the groups and discrediting the industry in the eyes of Maryland's resource managers.[20]

The industry's internal conflicts and the independent nature of watermen weaken the political effectiveness of the seafood industry. Unlike the farm groups discussed in chapter 4, commercial watermen associations have been far less successful in attempting to influence electoral politics. The National Institute on Money in State Politics database of political contributions reveals no political contributions from commercial watermen associations or seafood processors in Maryland or Virginia in recent elections.[21] Instead, these groups have relied on limited lobbying efforts and legal strategies for pursuing their political goals. Lobbying by watermen's associations is typically a grassroots activity that involves testifying at regulatory and legislative hearings or attempting to influence the broader political debate by making their case through the news media. And as a final resort after losing a regulatory battle, some groups have chosen to pursue legal action to try to block regulations.

While it would be a mistake to present the crab industry as a powerful political force, armed with campaign contributions and a stable of high-paid lobbyists, it would also be a mistake to underestimate the political clout that watermen and their associated groups possess. For example, in Maryland, several groups have effectively organized to protect crabbing interests, including groups that represent recreational crabbers like the Maryland Saltwater Fisherman's Association and the Conservation Corps of America. Maryland's commercial watermen have long benefited from the political know-how and energy of Larry Simns, president of the Maryland Watermen's Association since its founding in 1973. Simns, a lifelong waterman from Rock Hall on Maryland's Eastern Shore and charter boat business owner, has well-honed political skills and connections that run deep within Maryland's General Assembly. Under his leadership, the Maryland Watermen's Association has established county boards in each of Maryland's Bayside counties and maintains a year-round office and permanent staff in Annapolis. Simns is a ubiquitous presence at the state capital each winter and spring when the regulatory process heats up.[22]

While there is no equivalent to Larry Simns or the Maryland Watermen's Association in Virginia, nine regional associations represent crabbers in Virginia.[23] More important, the Virginia associations are given a central role in the state's regulatory process. As discussed earlier, Virginia's regulatory body, the Virginia Marine Resource Commission, is required by law to have at least one seat filled by a commercial waterman and another by a recreational fisherman. The state's other resource commissioners also tend to have close ties to fishing interests and watermen communities. In Virginia, unlike in Maryland, the need for a statewide organization within the industry is mitigated by the fact that watermen have an institutional presence in the regulatory process.

During these turbulent times for the crabbing industry, it is difficult to estimate the actual political clout that commercial fishermen and the seafood industry possess in Maryland and Virginia. At times they appear to be powerful political brokers, able to stave off regulatory pressures that threaten the short-term interests of their industry, though recently they have appeared far less effective at resisting the mounting body of evidence that suggests more aggressive management actions are necessary for the Bay. One thing is clear: the industry has been particularly poor at pursuing the types of creative management approaches that could reduce the crab harvest while simultaneously preserving the watermen's unique way of life. Strapped by limited resources and dwindling political capital, the groups have focused their attention on resisting regulations, an approach that has earned them a reputation as obstructionists within crab management circles and has further reduced their political influence.

DIVIDED GOVERNMENT AND BLUE
CRAB MANAGEMENT FOR THE BAY

Garrett Hardin's theory of "the tragedy of the commons," outlined in chapter 2, offers valuable insights into the problems facing blue crab management. While Hardin wrote of herdsmen overgrazing a common area, it takes little imagination to apply his theory to watermen and the overharvesting of the blue crab. Like the herdsmen in Hardin's example, watermen desire to maximize their individual profits. According to Hardin's logic, each waterman grapples with the following question, "What is the utility of harvesting one more crab?" For each waterman, there is both a positive and a negative aspect to increasing their harvest. The positive is that the individual waterman gains the profit, a benefit that the waterman enjoys individually. The negative is that taking an additional crab contributes to overharvesting; a negative effect shared by all waterman and recreational crabbers. With the individual waterman receiving all benefits and able to share the negative consequences, Hardin's logic suggests that the incentive is for watermen to overharvest the Bay's common crab stock. In other words, if unregulated, the short-term thinking of individual watermen would destroy the long-term health of the crab.[24]

More than just a powerful argument for natural resource management, Hardin's ideas have implications for multijurisdictional management problems such as those that face the Bay. As discussed earlier, local and state governments are reluctant to take actions that put industry in their area at an economic disadvantage to similar industries in surrounding areas. Like the herdsmen or watermen discussed previously, local and state governments enjoy individual benefits from the crabbing industry in their areas and are able share the burden of overharvesting with other jurisdictions. With each level of government interested in protecting their individual crabbing interests and no level of government desiring to provide economic advantages to other jurisdictions, intergovernmental competition acts as a powerful force against effective management of the crab.

These competitive forces have driven crab regulations in Maryland and Virginia for nearly a century. Resource managers in the two states have not only had to grapple with the issue of how regulations might influence the Bay's crab stock in general; they are also forced to consider how regulations might put the crabbing industry in their state at a competitive disadvantage to the industry in the other state. Overcoming these powerful competitive forces remains the single biggest challenge facing the Bay's resource managers.

Realizing the destructive influence of interstate competition, the Chesapeake Bay Commission has been advocating a Baywide approach of crab management for over two decades—in 1982, it sponsored a bistate workshop; in 1984, it convened the Bay's first Bi-State Fisheries Advisory Working Group; in 1987, it fought to make sure the Second Bay Agreement included Baywide management plans as a goal; and in 1996, it convened the Bi-State Blue Crab Advisory Committee (BBCAC), its latest attempt at Baywide management for the blue crab.

The Bi-State Blue Crab Advisory Committee currently has twenty-four members with representatives from all facets of the blue crab regulatory and stakeholder communities, including members from the

Chesapeake Bay Commission, Maryland's Department of Natural Resources, Virginia's Marine Resource Commission, watermen associations, the seafood-processing industry, Chesapeake Bay Foundation, Chesapeake Bay Program, and the Potomac River Fisheries Commission. The committee has formed a second group, the Technical Working Group (TWG), which includes twenty-nine of the leading crab researchers from Virginia and Maryland.

Guided by scientific research, the Bi-State Advisory Committee was able to achieve a consensus regarding the decline of the blue crab and establish the Baywide harvest reduction goal of 15 percent. The 15 percent reduction goal, set to be phased in between 2000 and 2003, was subsequently adopted by state agencies in both states, marking the first time that Virginia and Maryland worked together toward a common, tangible management goal for the blue crab. This common goal has helped to reduce the risks associated with unilateral regulatory action and has greatly diminished the negative effect of cross-state competition.

Though the influence of competition has been reduced by the actions of the Bi-State Commission, it has not been entirely overcome. The lack of regulatory coordination continues to pose obstacles for blue crab management. One example of the difficulties that remain occurred in March 2001, when the Virginia Marine Resource Commission, after agreeing in principle to the 15 percent reduction goal, voted unanimously to postpone issuing its 2001 crab regulations until April, so that it could see how Maryland chose to handle crab regulations that year. Given the economic stakes for Virginia watermen and the fierce opposition to new regulations in 2001, Virginia's "wait-and-see" approach was understandable. Quite simply, the state wanted to do as much but no more than was necessary, and certainly no more than Maryland. The hesitation suggests a continuation of the "lowest common denominator" management mentality that has plagued blue crab management for the Chesapeake.

THE POLICY CYCLE, FOCUSING EVENTS, AND POLITICAL LEADERS: MAKING THE MOST OF LIMITED OPPORTUNITIES FOR BLUE CRAB MANAGEMENT

It was not until the Bay's other major commercial fisheries had collapsed and a large body of evidence suggested the blue crab was in serious danger itself that the champions of sensible blue crab management were able to muster enough political support to make significant headway. In short, the many lessons of the Bay's failed fisheries, as poignant as they were, were insufficient to spur policymakers to take proactive management steps to protect the crab prior to its decline. It took blue crab harvests reaching record lows and a chorus of scientists warning of an impending collapse to spur government action.

By the year 2000, all indicators suggested the blue crab was in serious danger, which in turn focused media scrutiny and heightened public concern regarding the health of the crab population. The declining size of the annual harvests and findings from the annual crab surveys provided substantial evidence that the stock, in particular the population of breeding-age crabs, had declined severely throughout the decade. Most recent estimates show the population of breeding crabs has dropped roughly 80 percent from 1988 to 2002.

These disturbing trends translated into increased media attention, which fostered public concern and provided fertile ground for policy action. Figure 6.2 shows the number of newspaper stories in the two states that mentioned the blue crab between 1994 and 2001.[25] The figure reveals the increased media attention that blue crab issues received in recent years. In 1994, crab issues received only moderate media attention, with only 50 articles in the two states. In 1996, the year the Bi-State Blue Crab Advisory Committee was created, more than 200 related news stories were published. And when Virginia and Maryland stepped up their regulatory actions to protect the crab harvest in 2001, over 300 stories were published in state papers. The health of the blue crab had become a pressing concern of the general public across the region.

Declining crab numbers and increased public awareness, however, were not sufficient to guarantee protective steps. It would eventually take the leadership of numerous key officials, scientists, and citizens to achieve the policy advances recently approved in the two states. Though a comprehensive discussion of the many advocates for crab protection is impractical in this work, mentioning some of the key figures is worthwhile. The recent management successes would most likely not have taken place without the leadership of Ann Pesiri Swanson, executive director of the Chesapeake Bay Commission and chair of the Bi-State Blue Crab Advisory Committee's Technical Working Group. Swanson's leadership and technical understanding have helped to bring together the

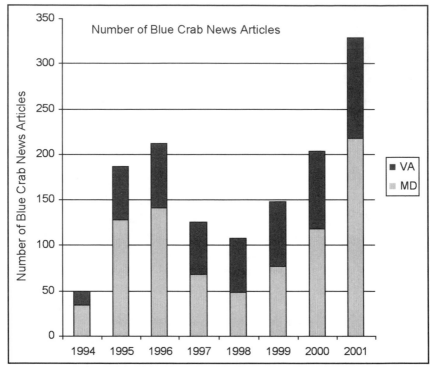

Figure 6.2.   Newspaper Coverage of the Blue Crab in Virginia and Maryland (1994–2001)
Source: **Calculated by the author from the Lexis-Nexis database.**

many marine researchers that comprise the Technical Working Group and produce the group's unprecedented consensus recommendations. Swanson's work earned her the title of Conservationist of the Year from the Chesapeake Bay Foundation in 2001. Other essential acts of political leadership have come from champions of crab management such as Maryland Governor Parris Glendening, who went so far as to push through regulations even when faced with substantial resistance from the General Assembly's oversight committee. Important leadership has also come from Maryland's recent secretaries of natural resources, who have each fought for more active crab management. Delegate John F. Wood (Maryland) and Delegate Robert S. Bloxom (Virginia), who co-chair the Bi-State Blue Crab Advisory Committee, have been particularly helpful in gaining legislative support. And over a dozen of the region's leading marine scientists have also contributed their expertise. In particular, Dr. Thomas J. Miller of the University of Maryland Chesapeake Biological

Laboratory provided essential leadership within the scientific community at key points in the crab management debate. These leaders, along with dozens of other dedicated advocates for sensible crab management, continue to struggle to overcome the substantial political obstacles that face blue crab management for the Chesapeake Bay.

CONCLUSION

It will be interesting to know whether, many years hence, we will read the most recent predictions, and place them alongside others from years past. Of course there is no way to know, and the precautionary path is the only sane one to take.

—Dr. Jack Greer (2002), Maryland Sea Grant College

Public concern and political leadership, grounded in science, have led to considerable action for the blue crab in recent years. Though consensus was slow to develop, Maryland and Virginia have been able to overcome many of their long-held differences and adopt common short-term reduction goals for blue crab management. The long-term outlook for the crab and the industry that it supports, however, remains unclear. Moving from common goals to a common regulatory strategy continues to elude resource managers in Maryland and Virginia, reducing the overall effectiveness of regulations in each state. Moreover, the management effort remains a reactionary enterprise, a response to the crab's dwindling numbers, rather than a proactive management endeavor.

It is too early to tell whether recent measures will be sufficient to protect the Bay's beautiful swimmers and whether sensible management will continue should the crab population rebound. The crab's heartiness and fecundity are perhaps its best hope for the future, though overreliance on its physical characteristics would be a mistake. Tropical storms, hurricanes, and the flooding that they can cause will occur in the region in the future. The crab's ability to survive these acts of nature is more and more a matter of human management decisions. With sensible harvesting levels and improved water quality, the crab is well suited to rebound from natural disturbances, as it has for millions of years. Without proper management and a healthy habitat, however, it may only be a matter of time before the population does in fact collapse.

Part IV

LEARNING FROM THE PAST

7

Toward a Brighter Future for the Chesapeake Bay

I hoped and prayed back in 1969 when I first started, that I'd be able to witness, once again, a healthy, vibrant Patuxent River and Chesapeake Bay. . . . I'm becoming a little more disillusioned. I'm not quite as optimistic as I was a few years ago that that will occur. . . . We are going to have to do something more dramatic than what we are doing at the present time if we're going to save the river and the Bay. Time just isn't on our side.

—Bernie Fowler (2001), former Maryland state senator

It does reach the point sometime where you have to have either mandatory regulations to get it done or a prohibitive ban on certain activities.

—Harry Hughes (2002), governor of Maryland 1979–1987

If resource managers were to sit down and design from scratch the ideal management structure for the Chesapeake Bay, it probably would not look very much like the structure that is currently in place. The Bay's bureaucracy has grown and evolved for nearly a century, responding to specific problems and taking advantage of limited political opportunities.[1] These reactions have been institutionalized in the current restoration bureaucracy. The most important question facing the restoration effort today is not whether there are a sufficient number of programs, but whether meaningful changes could be made to more fully empower those fighting for the Bay. In other words, what political reforms and strategies might be pursued not only to help Bay advocates respond to the crisis du jour, but also to successfully pursue the type of long-term planning that could head off future crises? If the Bay's environmental woes are inexorably linked to shortcomings in the political process, as this work argues, we must look to the political system for solutions. In this chapter, ten reform suggestions are put forth that attempt to address the Bay's political problems.

Recognizing the substantial accomplishments of the past and building upon the belief that even small changes can have a profound impact on policy outcomes, many of the suggestions that follow may appear relatively minor. Rebuilding the Bay's restoration machine from scratch would be as unwise as it is impractical, but greasing its wheels through modest reforms is an essential step in ensuring future environmental progress. While some of the reforms are structural and others are strategic, each reform suggestion is designed with the study's theoretical framework in mind. They are designed to either minimize the policy constraints identified in the study (i.e., economic primacy, interest group imbalance, and divided government) or to make the most of the policy cycle and periodic disturbances that provide opportunities for environmental policy leaders.

Perhaps the greatest challenge when considering reform options is how to bring about meaningful improvements without sacrificing the collaborative spirit and collegial atmosphere that permeates the Bay's restoration effort. As the program moves increasingly toward a regulatory approach, as it inevitably must to reach the next level of protection, it will remain important to maintain the goodwill that has fueled the collaborative effort to date. But a balanced approach requires that voluntary measures and economic incentives be complemented by meaningful regulations and ardent enforcement, a move that will undoubtedly sour some to the process.

TEN MEASURES TO IMPROVE POLITICS FOR THE BAY

1. A Bistate Approach to Managing the Bay's Living Resources

Resource management in Virginia and Maryland has slowly shifted from primarily a legislative responsibility to the responsibility of executive agencies. The Virginia Marine Resources Commission, which once served as an advisory commission to the Virginia General Assembly, has increasingly been delegated regulatory authority. Likewise, Maryland's Department of Natural Resources and the various commissions that preceded its creation in 1969 have also been delegated regulatory powers that were once reserved for the state's General Assembly. The power shift took place in both states for similar reasons: the part-time general assemblies of the states lack the resources to engage in the increasingly full-time job of resource management.

As the Chesapeake Bay restoration effort continues to evolve, it is time to seriously consider whether Baywide resource management would benefit from a similar evolution, from primarily advisory to regulatory. For example, the Bi-State Blue Crab Advisory Committee, which has been advising crab regulators in the two states since 1996, could be delegated increased managerial responsibilities, completing its evolution from an advisory to a regulatory commission. Or a new committee, a Chesapeake Bay Marine Resources Commission, which would manage each of the Bay's living resources from a Baywide perspective, could be created to bring coordinated resource management to the Bay.

Such a Baywide approach could function in a similar way as the Potomac River Fisheries Commission currently functions, with shared input from the resource managers of the two states and with the states sharing responsibility for enforcing its regulations. The obvious benefit of a Baywide regulatory commission is that it could minimize bistate competition for the Bay's resources. With a single regulatory authority in place, Bay managers would be better situated to pursue the rules that are necessary to protect the Bay's living resources and to spread the price of regulations equitably between the states. Moreover, it is likely that they would be better able to pursue the type of proactive management steps that are currently hampered by interstate competition, and, by doing so, reduce the necessity to take more restrictive measures in the future.

2. Controlling Pollutants: Welcoming the TMDL Approach

When passed in 1972, the federal Clean Water Act required that the EPA and the states enforce total maximum daily loads (TMDLs) for each pollutant entering the nation's waterways.[2] For each waterway, the Chesapeake Bay and its many tributaries included, water quality standards were to be set, sources of pollutants were to be identified, firm pollution limits were to be set, and pollution reduction plans were to be applied as needed.

If the level of pollutants entering a body of water exceeded the maximum allowed (i.e., reached a point that the body of water fell below the established water quality standards and became impaired), regulatory actions would be taken to address the sources of the pollutants.

The problem with the TMDL component of the Clean Water Act is that the states and the federal government have largely ignored it for three decades. For years, the EPA failed to issue rules that would move the process forward, and the states were slow to submit lists of impaired waters, making enforcement of TMDLs a nonissue. It was not until late in 1999, facing lawsuits in thirty-five states, that the EPA began to take the TMDL requirement seriously, issuing its much-anticipated final rules on TMDLs on July 13, 2000, which required states to develop implementation plans.[3] Legal actions also had far-reaching implications in Virginia and Maryland. Litigation in Virginia, brought by the American Canoe Association and the American Littoral Society, resulted in a 1999 consent decree that established a schedule for Virginia to develop TMDLs for its impaired waters through 2010. Under the consent decree, if Virginia fails to meet the schedule, the EPA is authorized to take control of the process and develop TMDLs for Virginia, as it has done in other states. In a similar suit in Maryland, a judge ruled in 2001 that the state was making sufficient progress in water quality improvement to satisfy Clean Water Act requirements and gave the state until 2011 to have the Bay removed from the EPA's list of impaired waters or to face TMDL requirements.

TMDLs hold a great deal of potential for the Bay and are likely to play a key role in improving water quality in the future. To date, the Chesapeake Bay restoration effort, with its focus on monitoring, nutrient reduction goals, and its emphasis on watersheds, has served as a nonregulatory form of a TMDL. Making the most of the TMDL authority afforded under the Clean Water Act, the restoration effort would be armed with regulatory sticks where it previously possessed only carrots. While the voluntary approach stressed in the past will undoubtedly continue to play a central part in the restoration effort, the fact remains that after more than twenty years of voluntary programs, the Chesapeake Bay and virtually all of it tributaries fail to meet the EPA's minimum water quality standards and are listed as impaired bodies of water. The difficult choices that lay ahead will require voluntary action *and* the full regulatory authority granted in the Clean Water Act, making TMDLs an essential facet of the future success of the Bay restoration effort.

3. Expanding the Role of the Chesapeake Bay Commission

One of the first steps in the Chesapeake Bay restoration effort was the creation in 1978 of the Chesapeake Bay Legislative Advisory Commission by the general assemblies of Virginia and Maryland. This commission was replaced by the Chesapeake Bay Commission in 1980, which was created to foster intergovernmental coordination in the management of the Chesapeake Bay. Since its creation, the Commission has issued dozens of studies and reports and has served as an indispensable policy advocate to the states, fighting for sensible public policy solutions for the Bay's environmental problems.

One area in which the Commission could better serve the Bay in the future would be to increase its federal presence. The Chesapeake Bay Commission's bylaws describe the organization's primary duties this way: "Identify specific Bay management concerns requiring intergovernmental coordination and cooperation and . . . recommend to the states and/or the federal and local governments legislative and administrative actions."[4] While the Commission is tasked with advising the federal government, its organizational structure does not facilitate such involvement. There are neither members of the U.S. Congress on the Commission nor representatives from the U.S. Environmental Protection Agency. Moreover, the Commission, which maintains offices in Pennsylvania, Maryland, and Virginia, does not operate a permanent office in Washington, D.C.

As the federal government's role in protecting the Bay continues to increase, the need for a more substantial Commission presence in Washington also grows. The federal government appropriates funds for the Chesapeake Bay Program, as well as several other federally funded projects.[5] Moreover, there are substantial funding opportunities available for the Bay through broader appropriation bills, such as the Farm Bill, transportation bills, wastewater treatment legislation, and education funding. The restoration effort will have to more successfully tap into these funding opportunities in the future in order to acquire the billions of dollars that are necessary to meet its goals.

The competition for federal funds beyond those allocated to all states through funding formulas is fierce, requiring political capital and innovative ideas.[6] One step the Commission could take to improve its ability to influence the federal process would be to include members of the EPA and members of Congress in the Commission. The representatives from the federal government could either serve alongside the state representatives, or they could form a separate unit of the Commission that specifically focuses on issues that require action by the federal government. Likewise, it would also benefit the effort if the Commission was able to establish a permanent office in Washington.

Another Commission-related reform could address the issue of political representation. Currently, only three of the six Bay states, Maryland, Pennsylvania, and Virginia, are represented on the Commission. Though these states comprise the bulk of the watershed and arguably have the most at stake in a clean Bay, they are not the only states that substantially influence the Chesapeake Bay ecosystem. Delaware, New York, and West Virginia each have land that falls within the Chesapeake Bay watershed, though none of these states has formal representation on the Chesapeake Bay Commission.[7] Short of having these states sign on as full Chesapeake Bay partners, which would likely give them more political representation on the Commission than their limited environmental influence on the Bay warrants, there are several options that could be explored to more actively involve these states in the Commission's work. One option might be to create a separate "Headwaters Commission" that addresses the unique problems facing the headwater sections of the Bay. Another option might be to include these states in a separate "Congressional Commission" so as to maximize the collective political strength of the watershed states at the national level, without endangering the effectiveness of the existing Commission. And yet another option would be to provide the excluded states limited representation on the existing Commission, perhaps representation in proportion to the amount of land that each state comprises in the watershed. In any case, finding an appropriate way to incorporate these states into the activities of the Chesapeake Bay Commission is an important issue that should receive more attention as the restoration partnership continues to develop and mature.

4. Expanding the Central Role of Water Quality Monitoring

As pollution caps are established in the future and enforced by regulatory measures, the role of monitoring will continue to grow in importance. For pollutant caps to work, it is imperative that regulators base their decisions on monitoring data that is beyond reproach. This is necessary from an environmental and a political perspective. Environmentally, monitoring provides the scientific feedback that is essential to adapt programs to the watershed's specific water quality problems. Reliable monitoring is equally necessary from a political perspective. The restrictions placed on industry and the general public to achieve pollution reduction goals will undoubtedly generate legal challenges. In order for the program to withstand the inevitable legal barrage, it will have to establish with scientific certainty that restrictions are necessary to comply with TMDL requirements.

The Chesapeake Bay Program's water-monitoring program was established in June 1984. The monitoring program was created primarily as a research tool to help resource managers learn more about the Bay as an ecosystem. When the Second Bay Agreement was signed in 1987 and the 40 percent nutrient reduction goal was established, the importance of water quality monitoring substantially increased. Since the 1987 Agreement, water quality monitoring has increasingly been used as an assessment tool by which pollution reduction efforts are measured.

In recent years, the Bay Program has annually spent between $1.5 and $2 million on assessment, employing six full-time people and issuing monitoring grants to Maryland and Virginia. Maryland and Virginia in turn match the Chesapeake Bay Program grants and hire research centers in each state to carry out the actual water-quality monitoring. Water quality for the main stem of the Bay is typically monitored at forty-nine locations, fourteen times per year. While the Program does not support monitoring in the nontidal tributaries that feed the Bay, it does make use of data from the states and other agencies that monitor these sights.

The Program's current monitoring regime is insufficient to meet the changing needs of Bay management. It could be compared to assessing the health of the Bay's human population by giving a few dozen people physical exams about once a month. The TMDL approach requires a far more expansive assessment program for each of the Bay's major tributaries, as well as an accurate measure of water quality throughout the main stem of the Bay. Realizing this, Carlton Haywood, the chair of the Chesapeake Bay Program's Monitoring and Analysis Subcommittee, has recently requested substantial increases in the Program's monitoring budget. Even with the $800,000 increase that the Bay Program's monitoring component was awarded for fiscal year 2003, it is unlikely that the Program will be able to keep pace with the restoration effort's growing monitoring needs.

Additional funds are necessary to put into practice permanent monitoring buoys, which can provide continuous monitoring of multiple areas throughout the Bay, and to fund the expanded use of towed monitoring equipment, which provides a spatial picture of the Bay's water quality at a given point in time. Additional funds will also be necessary to hire more analysts to process and interpret the increased data that is derived from the expanded monitoring system. Though improving the monitoring program will be an expensive undertaking, it is a fundamentally important step for the future success of the restoration program.

5. Taking the Initiative:
Circumventing the "Normal" Political Process

If, as this study suggests, public policy outcomes do not reflect the general public's concern for the environment, one way to promote more ambitious environmental policy would be to circumvent the traditional policy process and to give citizens a more active role in the process. This can be achieved in any number of ways, including through ballot initiatives, which place public policy issues on the ballot following a successful signature-gathering period, or through the referendum process, in which lawmakers refer policy issues to the voters for approval.[8]

Recent analysis offers strong support for the idea that people, given the chance, will support environmentally friendly public policy. Research by Phyllis Myers of the Brookings Institution found that voters approved 72 percent of the 240 land protection ballot measures that appeared on the ballot nationwide in 1998, committing more than $7.5 billion of state and local spending to conservation measures. In the year 2000, 553 land conservation ballot measures appeared on state and local ballots, with a passage rate of 72 percent.[9] Another study by the Trust for Public Land found similar high-passage rates for land conservation measures in recent years, even measures that require communities to increase taxes to preserve land.[10] The most ambitious conservation measure to date was approved by California voters in 2002, when voters in that state authorized a $2.6 billion bond measure to preserve the state's natural resources and to improve state and local parks.

Currently, statewide environmental ballot measures are not possible in Maryland and Virginia since the constitutions of these states do not allow for such measures.[11] In Virginia, a constitutional amendment that would have given its citizens the initiative and referendum process passed the House of Delegates in 1914, only to be killed in the senate. A similar amendment reintroduced fifty years later by gubernatorial hopeful Henry Howell and Fairfax Delegate Vincent Callahan was also killed.[12] In Maryland, the Maryland Direct Legislation League won passage of the legislative referendum in 1915. This reform gives Marylanders the ability to force legislation that has passed the General Assembly to be placed on the ballot for public approval. The process gives citizens a chance to veto unpopular laws and has been used seventeen times since authorized, but provides no mechanism for citizens to propose legislative changes, which severely limits its utility as an environmental policy tool.

While adopting the initiative and referendum in Maryland and Virginia would have ramifications far beyond environmental policy and should certainly not be viewed as an environmental policy panacea, these democratic processes would undoubtedly provide opportunities for environmental policy that is currently limited by the existing policy process. These legislative tools provide a more direct mechanism for translating the widespread public support that currently exists for the Bay into the type of Bay-friendly public policies that have been so difficult to pass through the conventional legislative processes. As advocates of the Bay consider political solutions for the Bay's environmental ills, careful consideration should be given to the tools of citizen governance.

6. Advocate or Abdicate:
Reinvigorating the Bay's Interest Group Community

The Chesapeake Bay Foundation (CBF) functions as the premier advocacy group for the Chesapeake Bay. It is by far the largest and most affluent group representing the Bay's environmental issues. Its success can be seen in the ubiquitous "Save the Bay" bumper stickers that grace automobiles throughout the watershed, in the organization's $11.6 million headquarters in Annapolis, and in the impressive array of properties that it owns throughout the region. The group enjoys the support of roughly a hundred thousand dues-paying members and the benefits that come with annual revenues that have topped $20 million in recent years.

It could be argued that the foundation's organizational success has been a mixed blessing for the Bay. On one hand, the group has been able to harness its impressive resources to serve as an environmental education leader for the region, helping to foster the environmental ethic upon which the restoration effort ultimately depends. On the other hand, with such a large constituency to satisfy, it is easy to see why the group might shy away from an aggressive political course, which could alienate parts of its membership base. Chesapeake Bay Foundation's political dilemma is a classic example of a group's organizational interests pulling it in one direction, toward political moderation, and its advocacy interests pulling it in another direction, toward political activism.

Today, the group's political activities do not reflect its substantial resources or its robust grassroots support. The group's 501(c)(3) nonprofit tax status limits its legal ability to engage in political activities, making political contribution and even political endorsements off-limits. To get around such restrictions, other prominent environmental organizations have traditionally operated under a divided structure, which allows part of a group to enjoy the benefits of nonprofit status while other facets of the group engage in political activities. For example, the Sierra Club's lobbying effort grew from that of one part-time lobbyist in the 1960s to a highly professional operation that employs nine full-time lobbyists. The club's political action committee (Sierra Club Committee on Political Education) has been active since 1976 and regularly contributes more than a quarter million dollars per election cycle to political candidates. The group also maintains a separate legal defense fund that allows the group to pursue its environmental objectives through the courts.[13] The Chesapeake Bay Foundation's decision to avoid such activities has severely limited its political relevance.

The foundation engages in relatively modest lobbying activities, operates no political action committee, and offers no political endorsements. The group has also chosen not to engage in "issue advertisement campaigns" that could apply public pressure to key policymakers throughout the political process. Likewise, the group's permanent legal staff has been reluctant to pursue the foundation's environmental objectives through the court system, considering this approach a last resort to be avoided if at all possible.[14] The foundation's political activities include a fairly ineffective "action network" that attempts to generate grassroots support for political issues by sending e-mail "alerts" to network subscribers, operating a modest phone bank, and periodically conducting training workshops to promote citizen activism for the Bay.

Other groups have attempted to fill the political void left by the Chesapeake Bay Foundation, but to date have only had limited success. Two groups, Clean Water Action and the League of Conservation Voters, have become increasingly active political players for the Bay. In particular, the Maryland League of Conservation Voters, considered the region's leader in political activity for the environment, has stepped up its efforts in recent years.[15] The group operates a modest political action committee, endorses candidates, evaluates the voting record of elected officials, and recruits environmentally friendly candidates for public office. The primary drawback to the league's political influence, and the influence of the Bay's other politically active groups, is its lack of resources. For instance, the Maryland League of Conservation Voters operated as a volunteer group for twenty years before opening a permanent office in 2000 and only has resources to fill three staff positions.

The Chesapeake Bay Foundation remains the only advocacy group with sufficient resources to launch a sustained political campaign for the Bay. While it is understandable that the group has been reluctant to dirty its hands in the political process, it is time for the organization's leadership to rethink their political strategy for the Bay. The future of the Bay depends on political action, and the Chesapeake Bay Foundation, as the region's leading environmental group, has a responsibility to be at the forefront of the political battle.

7. Making the Most of Disturbances

This study, like others before it, argues that major events or disturbances create policy opportunities that do not exist under normal conditions.[16] The theory suggests that environmental policy innovations are most likely to occur when environmental conditions are at their worst. It helps to explain why the path of environmental policy has tended to be reactive—a response to the latest crisis—rather than proactive and forward-looking. Appreciating the importance of political disturbances, and the opportunities they provide, might better prepare environmental advocates for the political fights that lay ahead.

At the most basic level, it is important that environmental groups organize in such a way that they can make the most of disturbances when they occur. Since the windows of opportunity provided by such events open for only brief periods of time, rarely more than a year, it is important for environmental groups to act fast to mobilize public interest and political leadership. The successful formation of ad hoc coalitions that bring together environmental groups, the scientific community, and affected industry groups in response to a disturbance event can mean the difference between policy success and failure. Such coalitions, such as the one that formed after the 1997 *Pfiesteria* scare, can attract sustained media coverage and provide political cover for policymakers, greatly increasing the chance of meaningful policy innovation.

Environmental advocates can also work to highlight regularly occurring environmental conditions that no longer receive sustained media attention. For example, it is well known that rainy conditions often lead to sewage leaks in the Baltimore area, a fact that receives little media attention considering the potential environmental and human health consequences of such leaks. A coordinated campaign by the area's leading environmental groups, complete with pictures and water quality samples, could bring attention to the problem. Likewise, large sections of the Bay experience hypoxic water conditions each summer, making them inhospitable for aquatic life. These "dead zones" have not been properly highlighted in recent years and, consequently, failed to cause the type of policy disturbance that they warrant. In short, a potential disturbance only becomes an actual disturbance if the environmental community successfully highlights the problem.

Environmental advocates also have a role to play in "manufacturing" disturbances. The results of scientific studies and lawsuits can produce disturbances in a similar way that an environmental tragedy can promote conditions that are conducive to policy innovation. The best example of this is the original EPA study of the Bay, completed in the early 1980s, which led to the creation of the Bay Program. Other examples include the recent legal action in Virginia, which forced that state to adopt a TMDL approach to water quality, and the 1978 lawsuit in Maryland, which helped to prompt the restoration effort for the Patuxent River. In each of these cases, environmental advocates took actions that challenged the conventional way of managing the Bay and triggered a series of events that fostered meaningful change.

8. From Dollars to Percents:
Rethinking the Cost of Environmental Restoration

In spring 2001, the Chesapeake Bay Foundation caused many people to stop and ponder the price of a saved Bay when it released the results of its study estimating that it would cost at least $8.5 billion to restore the Bay by 2010. The study brought much-needed attention to both the cost of future programs and the inadequacy of the existing spending levels. It boiled the Bay restoration effort down to one central question: how much is a vibrant Bay worth to the people of the Chesapeake Bay watershed?

From a political perspective, assigning a price tag to the restoration effort, especially one so daunting as $8.5 billion, causes many problems. At the very least, such a large figure may dissuade would-be supporters, making the restoration effort appear to be a desirable luxury that the region simply cannot afford. Moreover, the figure is also probably unrealistically low, creating the potential for a situation similar to the nutrient reduction goal fiasco of the late 1980s and 1990s, in which achieving "political success," in this case funding success, may not translate into environmental success.[17] Last, placing a fixed price on restoration promotes the notion that the cost of restoration represents a onetime expense, when in fact the price to restore and maintain the Bay requires a continuous public commitment.

While no one doubts the need for additional funds, the central political question remains, what is the best strategy for securing additional funds? One strategy might be to change the nature of the funding debate from dollars to percents. That is, while it may seem unreasonable for political actors to commit to a multi-billion-dollar campaign to restore the Bay, especially during tight budgetary times, it seems far more reasonable for policymakers to allocate just 1 percent of a state's budget to fund additional pollution reduction measures. If Maryland and Virginia were to set aside just 1 percent of their budgets to fund new restoration measures, it would translate into more than $400 million a year in additional revenue for the Bay, a figure that would grow substantially in future years as state budgets continue to increase. Over a ten-year period, it is likely that this ever-increasing amount, coupled with modest increases in federal funding and funding from other watershed states, would be sufficient to meet the funding gap identified by the Chesapeake Bay Foundation and others. These resources could be dedicated to a separate fund, a "Chesapeake Bay Environmental Trust Fund," that would protect the money during tight budgetary times. The funds could be used for major capital improvements, such as sewage treatment plant upgrades, and to help pay for other cash-strapped pollution control programs.

Pursuing a percentage-based strategy for Bay programs has at least two important political advantages to the traditional way people fight for fiscal resources. First, it reduces the matter to a manageable political issue. A candidate's support of "1 Percent for the Bay" could serve as a straightforward litmus test for his or her environmental commitment. Candidates would either endorse the commitment, or explain to the general public why much-needed capital improvements for the Bay are not worth 1 percent of the state budget. Second, the commitment reflects the continuous nature of environmental protection expenses. As a state's economy and public revenues grow, so too will the amount of money available for environmental capital improvements.

Today's environmental restoration program for the Bay, if successful, will eventually become tomorrow's environmental preservation program. In other words, the price of a clean Bay will not disappear, or even necessarily be reduced, should the restoration effort attain its goals. The expense of mitigating the environmental impact of modern life extends indefinitely into the future. With this in mind, it is essential that advocates for the Bay choose a funding strategy and political vocabulary that reflects the long-term environmental needs of the Bay.

9. Keeping the Bar High: Protecting Natural Processes and Native Resources

Policymakers in Virginia and Maryland are at a pivotal point in the restoration effort. They can either continue to address the underlying water quality and overharvesting issues that have contributed to the decline of the Bay's living resources, or they can pursue artificial means of making the Bay's living resources more resilient to the by-products of human activity. The traditional restoration approach stresses issues such as improving water quality, restoring wildlife habitat, guarding against disease, and achieving sustainable harvesting pressures. The new "resilience approach" moves the restoration effort in a different direction. This approach seeks to introduce robust nonnative or genetically engineered species to the Bay or to artificially bolster the Bay's native species through hatchery programs and other aquaculture techniques.

The Virginia Seafood Council, a trade group representing Virginia's seafood industry, has been pushing hard for a program that would introduce Asian oysters, *Crassostrea ariakensis,* to the Bay. This oyster is especially attractive to the seafood industry because it is resilient to diseases that have become common in the Bay, it grows quickly, and it tastes good.[18] Likewise, scientists at the University of Maryland's Biotechnology Institute have successfully bred crabs in their Baltimore laboratory, opening up the possibility of a blue crab hatchery program for the Bay. These researchers are able to promote year-round mating and hatching of crabs by manipulating laboratory conditions to simulate spring and summer days.

What is good news for the seafood industry is not necessarily good news for the Bay. The environmental consequences of such activities, especially introducing foreign species into the Bay, are difficult to anticipate and potentially profound. Foreign species compete with native species for limited habitat and alter the Bay's physical and biological composition in untold ways. Concerns regarding the potential environmental consequences of introducing foreign oysters have caused the Virginia Institute of Marine Science, the U.S. Fish and Wildlife Service, and the Chesapeake Bay Program to call for more research before the project continues. Quite simply, environmental scientists are unsure what impact Asian oysters might have on the Bay's other living resources and on resources beyond the Bay as the species spreads.

The *political* consequences of pursuing foreign species and aquaculture are far more predictable. These quick fixes divert attention and resources from the Bay's depleted condition and work to lower the bar for the restoration effort. If foreign oysters can thrive in the Bay's polluted waters, the political force behind improving water quality is weakened. Likewise, if hatcheries can artificially introduce millions of new crabs to the Bay each year, the effort to restore aquatic grasses, protect egg-bearing females, and control overharvesting practices loses its political force.

The introduction of foreign oysters, hatchery-raised crabs, and the like are not restoration measures; they are admissions of failure. To "restore" is to bring back what once was, not to introduce foreign species or adopt artificial processes. It is time for the environmental community to voice its opposition to this potentially dangerous management trend.

10. A Legal Strategy for the Bay: The Role of the Judicial System

Tom Horton, the Bay's premier environmental author, is fond of saying that he cannot think of any advances in environmental protection that "have not come from court cases or the threat of court cases."[19] Horton is correct to cite the importance of legal action in the restoration process. It was legal action during the late 1970s that caused Maryland to implement biological nutrient removal technology on the Patuxent River. It was legal action that forced the EPA and the state of Virginia to enforce the TMDL requirements of the Clean Water Act. And it was legal action that forced the city of Baltimore more recently to commit nearly a billion dollars to improve its failing sewage system.

In Maryland's 2002 legislative session, the General Assembly approved legislation that promises to make legal action an even more important part of protecting the state's natural resources. This legislation makes it easier for citizens and groups to legally challenge environmental permits issued by the state. Under the Environmental Standing Act of 1978, Marylanders had to satisfy "proprietary interest" criteria, which required them to show that issuing an environmental permit would cause harm to their person or property that was greater than harm caused to the general public. The revised standing requirement, adopted in 2002, relaxes the criteria, making it easier for people to seek judicial review of Maryland Department of the Environment's permit decisions.

While Maryland's new standing requirement is no silver bullet, it can be used to help pursue a more aggressive legal strategy for the Bay, one that will undoubtedly play a large role in the future of the restoration effort. For legal action to be more influential in the future, advocates for the Bay will need to overcome the stigma that has come to be associated with environmental lawsuits. The Bay restoration effort, with its strong emphasis on collaboration and its close network of political actors, fosters an environment that is generally not conducive to legal action. While industry interests have no qualms about protecting their legal rights through the courts, whether it is the watermen protecting their fishing rights or agriculture industries resisting environmental regulations, the environmental community, ever sensitive not to appear unreasonable, has come to devalue legal action. The consequence is a legal double standard that can, if perpetuated, afford greater legal protections to industry interests than it does to advocates of environmental protection.

CONCLUSION

In dealing with the State we ought to remember that its institutions are not aboriginal, though they existed before we were born; that they are not superior to the citizen; that every one of them was once the act of a single man; every law and usage was a man's expedient to meet a particular case; that they all are imitable, all alterable; we may make as good; we may make better.

—Ralph Waldo Emerson (1876), "Politics"

Emerson's quote reminds us of the practicality of the political process. Laws, programs, and reforms that fall short of their intended goals can and should be modified or replaced with more promising alternatives. Existing political structures represent nothing more than the latest attempt to achieve society's common goals, and they receive their value from their ability to promote these goals. As the region's political system continues to grapple with environmental protection, it is important not to adjust environmental goals to reflect "political realities" or to grow content with hollow "successes" that fail to reflect tangible environmental improvements. It is politics that must adapt to society's ever-changing needs. Through a more effective political strategy, we may yet secure a brighter future for the Chesapeake Bay.

Nutrient Management and the Bay

Year	Progress?	Regress?
1972	*Federal government passes the Clean Water Act (CWA).* The goal of the Clean Water Act is "to restore and maintain the chemical, physical, and biological integrity of the nation's waters." CWA left it up to the states to monitor water quality, develop standards, and implement standards. *Federal government passes the Coastal Zone Management Act (CZMA).* The intent of the legislation is to protect coastal areas by establishing partnerships between federal and state governments. The federal government provides funds for states to implement programs that are consistent with federal coastal management goals.	*Loss of wetlands.* From the mid-1950s to the late 1970s, more than 2,800 acres of Bay wetlands are lost to development each year. *Tropical Storm Agnes.* This storm causes record flooding and nutrient loads to the Bay, resulting in heightened concern among environmental scientists. *Bay grasses suffer from nutrient loading.*
1973		*Corps of Engineers study of the Bay identifies nutrients as a*

(continued)

Year	Progress?	Regress?
		primary factor degrading the Bay's water quality.
1975	*U.S. Senator Charles Mathias gains EPA funding for Bay study.* The EPA is awarded twenty-five million dollars to complete a five-year study of the health of the Chesapeake Bay.	
1977	*Federal government passes the Clean Air Act (CAA).* Enacted to improve the nation's air quality. Recent research suggests that fully enacting CAA and its subsequent amendments could substantially reduce nutrient overenrichment resulting from atmospheric pollution.	
1978	*EPA launches multiyear study of the Bay's health.*	
1980	*Chesapeake Bay Commission created.* The commission is created to advise the general assemblies of Virginia, Maryland, and the U.S. Congress on environmental matters related to the Bay.	
1981	*Scientists and environmental groups take legal action.* Lawsuit filed against state and federal environmental officials over plans to substantially increase the amount of wastewater from sewage treatment facilities released to the Patuxent River.	*Population growth.* Between 1950 and 1980, population in the Chesapeake Bay basin increases almost 50 percent (8.3 million to 12.4 million). *Land development.* Between 1950 and 1980, the amount of land used for residential and

Year	Progress?	Regress?
	First biological nutrient removal plant created. Legal settlement over sewage treatment along the Patuxent River leads to implementation of the area's first biological nutrient removal system.	commercial purposes increases by 180 percent (from 1.5 million acres to 4.2 million acres).
1983	*EPA Bay report completed.* The EPA identifies nutrient reduction as one of the most important actions necessary to restore the Bay.	*EPA Bay report.* This report finds the health of the Bay to be rapidly deteriorating.
	Maryland Governor Harry Hughes forms the Wye Group. This group of public officials is assembled to discuss ways to address the problems identified by the recently released EPA study.	
	First Bay Agreement. Bay states formally commit to Bay restoration.	
	Chesapeake Bay Program established. From the outset, the Program identifies nutrient reduction as a top priority for the Bay.	
1984	*Water quality–monitoring program created.* The Bay Program initiates a water quality–monitoring program.	*Agricultural stipulations to critical use laws in Maryland.* Despite the known negative impact of many modern farming practices, Maryland's protective land development law, establishing a 100-foot protective buffer against Bayside development, reduces the buffer
	Maryland passes Critical Areas Protection Act. The act seeks to control development in Maryland along the shore and tributaries of	

(continued)

Year	Progress?	Regress?
	the Bay to preserve natural nutrient and pollution buffers.	to only 25 feet for agriculture land.
1985	*Maryland phosphate detergent ban enacted.* *Pennsylvania joins the Chesapeake Bay Commission.*	*Nitrogen loading from septic tanks.* Ten million pounds of nitrogen per year enters the Bay from septic tanks.
1986	*Scientific and Technical Advisory Committee Report completed.* This report finds compelling evidence that both nitrogen and phosphorous reductions are needed to improve water quality in the Bay. *D.C. phosphate detergent ban enacted.* *First nutrient management plans established.* The Bay Program begins its first nutrient management efforts. These are voluntary plans designed to help landowners reduce nonpoint source nutrients entering the Bay from their land.	
1987	*Clean Water Act amended.* The 1972 Clean Water Act is amended and strengthened, calling on states to implement nonpoint source and point source nutrient reduction technologies. *Task force recommendation given.* A task force of scientists recommends a 40 percent reduction of nutrients entering the Bay as the minimum reduction	*Growth of industrial agriculture.* The size of the average chicken farm in Pennsylvania grows 100-fold from 1,000 chickens (1954) to 100,000 chickens (1987). Similar increases are taking place in Maryland and Virginia and in other types of farming (e.g., milk cows and hogs). *Chesapeake Bay Program interpretation of the Bay*

Year	Progress?	Regress?
	necessary to restore the Bay's living resources. *Second Bay Agreement effected.* Establishes a goal of reducing by at least 40 percent the nutrients entering the Bay by the year 2000.	*Agreement.* Chesapeake Bay Program sets the goal of reducing 40 percent of "controllable" nutrients.
1988	*Virginia phosphate detergent ban enacted.* *Virginia passes the Chesapeake Bay Preservation Act.* A legislative act championed by Governor Baliles designed to assist local governments in the implementation of state environmental regulations.	*Concentration of industrial agriculture.* Farming continues to intensify in concentrated areas throughout the watershed, including Lancaster County (PA), Eastern Shore (MD), and Rockingham County (VA). *Agricultural stipulations to protective land use laws in Virginia.* Virginia's protective land development law, designed to provide land use guidance to local governments, provides exemptions for approved agricultural practices. *Automobile usage outpaces population growth.* In 1976, 466,000 vehicles a day made use of the Capitol Beltway; by 1988, the number increases to 735,000.
1989	*Maryland Nutrient Management Program established.* The program is a voluntary nutrient reduction program designed to help farmers reduce agricultural nonpoint source nutrient pollution in Maryland.	

(continued)

Year	Progress?	Regress?
1990	*Federal government passes amendments to the Clean Air Act.* If fully implemented, the amendments should help to curb atmospheric nitrogen in the Bay area.	*Population growth continues.* Population in the watershed passes 13 million. Areas of highest growth tend to be concentrated in counties adjacent to the Bay.
	Pennsylvania phosphate detergent ban enacted.	*Agricultural exemptions to sediment control laws.* State laws in each of the Bay states exempt agricultural practices, such as plowing, from the permit requirements of their sediment control laws.
1992	*Tributary strategy established.* Amendments to the 1987 Bay Agreement direct the Chesapeake Bay Program to adopt a tributary strategy, attempting to reduce nutrients at their source.	
	Nutrient management plans grow. By 1992, the EPA estimates that nearly half a million acres of land in the Bay watershed are under nutrient management plans.	
1993	*Pennsylvania passes nutrient management law.* Pennsylvania passes the PA Nutrient Management Act and becomes the first Bay state to move toward mandatory nutrient management plans for high-density animal operations.	
	Chesapeake Executive Council speaks. The council issues a directive concerning agricultural nonpoint source pollution.	

Year	Progress?	Regress?
1994	*Bay state initiatives formed.* Signatories of the Bay Agreement outline initiatives designed to reduce nutrients entering the Bay's tributaries.	*Vehicle miles traveled.* From 1970 to 1994, vehicle miles traveled in the watershed increases 105 percent. *Increase in electricity use.* From 1960 to 1994, electricity usage in the region increased 400 percent. Utility industries produce roughly 50 percent of the airborne nitrogen oxide in the area. Over 20 percent of the total nitrogen pollution entering the Bay each year comes from atmospheric nitrogen.
1995	*Local government partnership initiative created.* Recognizing the importance of local decisions for Bay restoration, Chesapeake Bay Program launches a program to involve the watershed's 1,650 local governments.	*Pennsylvania fails to create regulations for its 1993 Nutrient Management Law.* Pennsylvania's Conservation Commission fails to draft agricultural management regulations by the two-year deadline specified in its 1993 Nutrient Management Law.
1996	*Riparian forest buffers initiative made.* This calls for the conservation of existing forests along the Bay's shores to serve as nutrient buffers, natural barriers limiting nutrient runoff from the land.	*High nutrient loads.* Heavy winter snows and Hurricane Fran lead to record high water flows into the Bay and massive nutrient loading. *Nitrogen loading from septic tanks continues to increase.* The annual nitrogen load from septic tanks reaches nearly 12 million pounds. *Omega Protein Corp.* The corporation borrows $20.5 million through a federal loan

(continued)

Year	Progress?	Regress?
		program to modernize its fishing and processing facilities used to harvest the Atlantic menhaden, one of the Bay's most plentiful fish species which is credited with consuming 25 percent of the Bay's nitrogen.
1997		*Failure to pass mandatory nutrient management plans in Virginia and Maryland.*
		Pennsylvania creates watered-down regulations for its 1993 Nutrient Management Law two years after the deadline. The regulations that emerge from Pennsylvania's much-touted legislation are estimated to only cover 5 to 10 percent of Pennsylvania farms and are roundly criticized by the environmental community.
		Amount of developed land continues to increase. From 1992 to 1997, the amount of developed land increases 15 percent in Virginia, 16 percent in Maryland, and 17 percent in Pennsylvania.
		Continued growth of poultry industry. The EPA reports that the poultry industry of the Delmarva Peninsula on Maryland's Eastern Shore houses 623 million chickens, which annually produce 3.2 billion pounds of waste containing 13.8 million pounds of phosphorous

Year	Progress?	Regress?
		and 48.2 million pounds of nitrogen.

Pfiesteria Piscicida. High nutrient level leads to toxic outbreaks of *Pfiesteria,* causing fish kills and potentially harming human health.

1998 — *Maryland passes mandatory nutrient management legislation (Water Quality Improvement Act)* Maryland farmers are called on to develop nutrient management plans by the end of 2001 and to implement the plans in future years or otherwise face penalties.

Wastewater treatment emphasized. Forty-three major municipal wastewater plants begin to implement biological nutrient reduction technologies, treating 31 percent of the Bay's municipal wastewater.

Population growth continues. Population in the watershed passes 15 million. Conservative estimates predict over 18 million people will reside in the watershed by 2020.

Increased pressure on menhaden. Since the 1970s, the average annual landings of menhaden tripled to approximately 300 million pounds per year. Pressure on menhaden, which eat large quantities of algae, is seen as a factor increasing algae concentrations in the Bay, aggravating a problem that was already on the rise due to nutrient overenrichment.

2000 — *Raw sewage.* Leaks and overflows from sewage systems are reported to have leaked millions of gallons of raw sewage into the Bay's tributaries.

40 percent nutrient reduction goal unrealized. The thirteen-year effort to reduce controllable nitrogen loads and controllable

(continued)

155

Year	Progress?	Regress?
		phosphorous loads by 40 percent comes up short by the 2000 goal.
2001	*Governor Glendening (MD) creates a task force to study the raw sewage leakage problem.*	*Bernie Fowler's annual "Wade-In."* Fowler finds water clarity on the decline in the Patuxent River for the second straight year.
		Loopholes to Maryland's Critical Areas Law. In the wake of three unfavorable court decisions, Governor Glendening (MD) claims loophole in Maryland's Critical Areas Law "big enough to drive development tractors through."
		Bay health on the decline. Chesapeake Bay Foundation's annual *State of the Bay Report* concludes the health of the Bay is on the decline.
		Maryland's 1998 Water Quality Improvement Act proves ineffective. At the deadline for Maryland farmers to submit nitrogen management plans, only 20 percent of the state's 1.7 million acres of farmland are under nutrient management plans.
2002	*Baltimore City commits to spend $900 million to update sewage system.* The EPA and the Department of Justice, using the threat of a lawsuit, pressure Baltimore to update its sewage system. The compromise gives	*Funding for Environmental Protection Programs cut.* Facing budgetary shortfalls, Maryland, Pennsylvania, and Virginia reduce spending for several environmental restoration programs.

Year	Progress?	Regress?
	the city fourteen years to complete the updates.	*Maryland farmers lobby for extension from the state's BMP requirements.*
		Pennsylvania's regulatory BMP law criticized as poorly executed.
		Over 900 sewage overflows in Baltimore. Reports show that Baltimore's sewage treatment system has resulted in over 900 overflows and an estimated 190 million gallons of sewage entering the Bay since 1996.

Notes

INTRODUCTION

1. Earnest Haeckel is credited with coining the phrase (Worster 1973, 3).
2. See Nash (1974, 1982, 1988, 1990), Coyle (1957), and Switzer (1994, ch. 1) for important works that discuss the history of environmentalism in the United States.
3. Switzer (1994, 4).
4. Davison et al. (1997, 36).
5. Environmental Protection Agency (1992).
6. Davison et al. (1997, 46).
7. See Davison et al. (1997, ch. 4) for a thorough description of Baltimore's environmental condition during the nineteenth century.
8. See Jones (1965) for a description of the creation of the Sierra Club and Switzer (1994, ch. 2) for an overview of early environmental groups.
9. See Ayres and Kneese (1969) for a classic work on externalities and economic systems.
10. See Vig and Kraft (1997, ch. 1) and Rosenbaum (1998) for more on environmental policy during this period.
11. See Lindstrom and Smith (2001) for a comprehensive account of the National Environmental Policy Act of 1970.
12. Rosenbaum (1998, 83).
13. The federal government enacted the Water Pollution Control Act as early as 1956 and additional clean air and water acts in the 1960s (i.e., Clean Air Act of 1963 and the Clean Water Act of 1965). However, it was not until after the creation of the EPA and passage of the clean air and water acts of the 1970s that the federal government assumed its dominant role in environmental protection.
14. Vig and Kraft (1997, 4).

15. See Rabe (1997) for a discussion of the decentralized nature of environmental politics.

16. See Favero (1997) for a work that takes a case study approach to explain environmental politics in the Chesapeake Bay.

17. See Switzer (1994, 174–75) for a brief history of the environmental politics of the Great Lakes.

1
THE CHESAPEAKE BAY:
MANAGEMENT OF NORTH AMERICA'S LARGEST ESTUARY

1. During the Pleistocene period sea levels were roughly 100 meters (325 feet) lower than they are today. For a concise geological history of the Chesapeake Bay region, see Fisher and Schubel (2001) and White (1989).

2. See Steadman (2001) for a list and the natural history of birds and mammals of the Chesapeake Bay region during the late Pleistocene and early Holocene periods.

3. The introduction of humans into the area at the very time that many large mammals were eliminated from the region has led some scholars to contend that overhunting by the North American Indians was the first widespread human impact on the Bay. See Martin and Klein (1984) for more on this topic.

4. Horton and Eichbaum (1991, 20).

5. The widest point of the Bay is Smith Point, Virginia.

6. See Horton and Eichbaum (1991, ch. 1) or Davison et al. (1997, ch. 2) for excellent descriptions of the Bay's physical characteristics.

7. Environmental Protection Agency (2000, 3).

8. White (1989, 3).

9. While many rivers and streams feed the Bay, the Bay's three largest rivers (i.e., Susquehanna, Potomac, and James) provide more than 80 percent of the Bay's fresh water (see Pritchard and Schubel 2001, 62). The U.S. Department of the Interior (2000) estimates that these three rivers contribute an average of about 19 trillion gallons of water to the Bay per year.

10. Generally speaking, the Bay is saltier in the fall during the dry season than it is in the spring when river flows tend to increase.

11. See Horton and Eichbaum (1991, 13–17) for a description of the complex nature of the Bay's water.

12. White (1989, 3).

13. Mencken (1940).

14. Chesapeake Bay Authority (1933, 23).

15. Chesapeake Bay Authority (1933, 23).

16. Chesapeake Bay Authority (1933, 18).

17. Steadman (2001, 99).

18. Beatty and Mulloy (1940).
19. See Davison et al. (1997) for an account of programs related to the restoration of the Chesapeake Bay.
20. See chapter 6 for more regarding this historic meeting.
21. See Chesapeake Bay Authority (1933) for the complete proceedings of the conference.
22. Quoted in Chesapeake Bay Authority (1933, 9).
23. Quoted in Chesapeake Bay Authority (1933, 176–77).
24. See Chesapeake Bay Authority (1933, 165–68).
25. The original legislation authorized $6 million for the study (see Section 312 of the River and Harbor Act of 1965). An additional $9 million was authorized in 1970 (see Section 3 of the River Basin Monetary Authorization Act of 1970).
26. The Hydraulic Model, which was commonly referred to as "the Monster of Matapeake" (the Maryland city in which it was housed), yielded few scientific findings and was closed in 1983. The concrete structure was 1,000 feet long, 21 inches deep at its deepest point, and held around 450,000 gallons of water. One of the last experiments conducted with the Hydraulic Model was to estimate the location of debris and human remains following the 1982 airline crash into the Potomac River. See Davison et al. (1997, 158–60) for more on the Hydraulic Model.
27. The Chesapeake Bay Commission was authorized through legislative action in each of the three states. See the Annotated Code of Maryland, Natural Resources Article, sec. 8-302; the Code of Virginia, Title 62.1, ch. 5.2, secs. 62.1-69.5 through 62.1-69.20; and Laws of Pennsylvania, Act 25 of 18985, 32 P.S. sec 820.11.
28. The 1983 Chesapeake Bay Agreement is posted on the Chesapeake Bay Program's website: www.chesapeakebay.net/overview.htm.
29. The 1987 and 2000 Chesapeake Bay Agreements are posted on the Chesapeake Bay Program's website: www.chesapeakebay.net/overview.htm.
30. See Chesapeake Bay Commission (2000) for a detailed explanation of the 2000 Bay Agreement.
31. Funding information was obtained from Marx (1999, 43) for the fiscal years 1984 through 1999. Information for fiscal years 2000 and 2001 was obtained from the Chesapeake Bay Commission (2001a, 10).
32. Chesapeake Bay Commission (2001a).
33. This number was calculated by dividing Maryland Department of Natural Resources' estimate for total state spending 2003–2010 (i.e., $4.41 billion) by the number of years included in the estimate (i.e., 7). See Maryland Department of Natural Resources (2002b, 7).
34. The amount that the other signatory states (Pennsylvania and Virginia) dedicate to Bay restoration programs is currently unavailable.
35. The Chesapeake Bay Foundation estimates it will cost $1 billion to upgrade sewage treatment plants, $2 billion to expand forest buffers, $2 billion

for land conservation, $1 billion to improve urban storm water infrastructure, $2 billion to implement farmland quality plans, and $500 million to restore wetlands and oysters. See Chesapeake Bay Foundation (2001a).

36. See Maryland Department of Natural Resources (2002b) and Blankenship (2002c) for more recent estimates.

37. Chesapeake Bay Program (1999c, introduction).

38. Horton (2001, 9).

39. Horton and Eichbaum (1991, 36).

40. See Horton and Eichbaum (1991) for a comprehensive analysis of the health of the Chesapeake Bay.

41. Leach, Pelkey, and Sabatier (2000).

42. Leach et al. (2000, 2).

43. Chesapeake Bay Commission (2001b, 15).

44. See Davison et al. (1997, ch. 7) for a description of oyster management practices in Maryland and Virginia waters.

45. See the Chesapeake Bay Program (1999c, 14) for more on the declining oyster harvest.

46. Newell (1988).

47. Horton and Eichbaum (1991, 27–29).

48. For more on the use of submerged aquatic grasses as a barometer of water quality , see Dennison et al. (1993).

49. Chesapeake Bay Program (1999a, 3).

50. Lynch (2001).

51. Chesapeake Bay Foundation (2002a).

52. There are numerous ways to monitor the health of the Bay's blue crab population, each of which has its own advantages and disadvantages. This study does not choose between the methods, but instead reports the general trend. See Chesapeake Bay Program (1995b, 38) for more on the various monitoring techniques.

53. National Oceanic and Atmospheric Administration (2001).

54. Bi-State Blue Crab Advisory Committee (2001c).

55. Chesapeake Bay Foundation (2000c, 4)

56. Horton and Eichbaum (1991, 31).

57. Alewife is commonly referred to as river herring.

58. Davison et al. (1997, 80).

59. The shad is an example of an anadromous species: it travels from the sea into the Bay's rivers to spawn. Since the shad spends a large part of its life outside the Bay, many factors other than the health of the Bay may be responsible for its reduction in numbers.

60. Chesapeake Bay Foundation (2002b).

61. The thirteen environmental categories include wetlands, forest buffers, underwater grasses, resource lands, toxics, water clarity, nitrogen, phosphorus, dissolved oxygen, crabs, rockfish, oysters, and shad.

2
THE CHESAPEAKE BAY AS A POLITICAL DILEMMA: UNDERSTANDING THE POLITICAL BARRIERS TO ENVIRONMENTAL POLICY

1. See Sabatier (1991) for an excellent assessment of leading public policy theories.

2. See Sabatier (1991) for a work that critiques the tendency of public policy research to focus on description rather than theory.

3. See Kraft (2001, ch. 3) for a summary discussion of theories related to environmental policy.

4. For a more optimistic account of environmental public policy, see Vig and Kraft (1997, ch. 1).

5. ABC News/*Washington Post* survey conducted April 19 through April 22, 2001, by TNS Intersearch; 1,350 adults surveyed; margin of error +/– 2.5 percent (release, April 24, 2001).

6. Bloomberg survey conducted May 29 through June 3, 2001, by Princeton Survey Research Associates; 1,208 adults surveyed; margin of error +/– 3 percent (release, June 6, 2001).

7. Potomac Inc. survey conducted January 1 through January 4, 2002; 800 registered voters surveyed; margin of error +/– 3.5 percent.

8. In 1998, 126 measures passed (84 percent), allocating $8.3 billion. In 1999, 92 measures passed (90 percent), allocating $1.8 billion. In 2000, 174 measures passed (83 percent), allocating $7.5 billion. In 2001, 137 measures passed (70 percent), allocating $1.7 billion. See the Trust for Public Land (2002).

9. Presidential adviser and democratic operative James Carville popularized the phrase "it's the economy, stupid" in 1992 and used it as the central theme for Bill Clinton's first presidential campaign.

10. This is not to say that voters ignore environmental issues at the polls; certainly, some Americans vote based on the environmental record of elected officials. However, the importance of general economic conditions on voting decisions has been well established, while the aggregate influence of environmental conditions has never been shown to have a significant impact on voting decisions in this country.

11. See Eisinger (1988) for a work that illustrates the economic connection between business and state politics.

12. For more about the impact of "cost-benefit" analysis, see *Economic Analysis at the EPA: Assessing Regulatory Impact*, edited by Morgenstern (1997).

13. See Miller (2001, 44–47) for more on the EPA under the Reagan presidency.

14. See 46 Federal Register 13193; CFR, February 17, 1981.

15. For a relevant example of this problem, see Castillo, Morris, and Raucher (1997). This case study discusses the tangible economic costs and the less tangible environmental benefits of the 1990 Clean Water Act amendments that promulgated the Great Lakes Water Quality Guidance for each of the states in the region. The EPA's regulatory impact analysis estimated that the cost (borne mostly by municipal and industrial facilities) could approach $376 million. This cost would have direct financial impact on established industries. For instance, the EPA estimated that the per-plant cost for the paper industry could reach $1.58 million. The ecological benefits, however, were much more difficult to quantify. The benefits included intangibles such as recreational fishing, the impact on wildlife observers and photographers, and the nonuse ecological value of a resource (i.e., its value beyond the direct human benefits that a resource provides).

16. See Connelly and Smith (1999, ch. 5) for a description of environmental valuation practices.

17. Several studies have shown the economic cost of environmental policy. For more on this topic, see Bacot and Dawes (1997); Davis (1992); and Feiock and Rowland (1991). For a recent study that challenges the commonly held notion that environmental protection necessarily hampers economic development, see Feiock and Stream (2001).

18. Rosenbaum (1998, 26) reports similar figures.

19. See Teitenberg (1994) for a study that questions the adverse economic effects of environmental public policy.

20. The Chesapeake Bay Foundation estimated that Bay restoration would cost a minimum of $8.5 billion, while more recent estimates place the figure at $7 billion for Maryland alone and close to $9 billion for Virginia (Blankenship 2002b, 2002c), with the other four Bay states and the District of Columbia also requiring sizeable contributions.

21. See Collins (2000) for an excellent discussion of the tragedy of the commons and the Chesapeake Bay's blue crab fishery.

22. See Mathew Crenson's (1971) work, *The Un-Politics of Air Pollution: A Study of Non-Decisionmaking in the Cities,* for an insightful work that explores the difficulties of passing environmental regulation at the local level. See Peterson (1981) for a more general work that illustrates how local governments compete for economic growth. See Miller (2001, ch. 6) for a recent work that considers federal environmental policy and state politics.

23. See Duerksen (1983) for an early work on the effects of governmental competition on environmental policy, Engel (1997) for a more recent and comprehensive look at the subject, and Potoski (2001) for a work that challenges the "race to the bottom" thesis.

24. See Engel (1997), a recent study that supports this thesis, and Ringquist (1993) and Lester (1994) for two studies that favor the role of states in environmental protection.

25. Maryland, in comparison, comprises only 15 percent of the Bay's drainage basin. Pennsylvania's chief river, the Susquehanna River, alone contributes roughly half of the Bay's freshwater. See EPA (1988b) for a comparative perspective.

26. See Miller (2001, ch. 8) and Switzer (1997) for two recent works about the organized opposition to environmental policy.

27. See McCloskey (1992) for an account of the successes and failures of the environmental movement in the United States. See Schlozman and Tierney (1986) and Furlong (1997) for two works that explore the relative strength of business groups compared to environmental groups.

28. Another important interest group that has a long history of working for Bay restoration is the Alliance for the Chesapeake Bay. For a directory of over 300 groups organized around Bay issues, see Chesapeake Bay Program (2002c).

29. See Chesapeake Bay Foundation (1998) and Horton and Eichbaum (1991) for historical overviews of the organization.

30. Chesapeake Bay Foundation (2000a).

31. While CBF's tax status as a 501(c)(3) organization limits its ability to legally engage in political activities, large advocacy groups such as CBF often have subsidiary groups not directly connected to the main group that more actively engage in political activities. CBF has chosen not to pursue this approach.

32. Hirshfield's primary responsibilities at CBF were to head its lobbying and litigation activities.

33. From Shultz (2002) and Hirshfield (2002) interviews.

34. The year 1998 was a gubernatorial election year in Maryland, which partially explains why contributions were comparatively larger in Maryland that year.

35. See Peters and Hogwood (1985) for an empirical study that tests the Downsian model.

36. Downs (1972, 38). See also Kingdon (1984) for another prominent work that discusses the idea of "windows of opportunity" for public policy development.

37. Downs (1972, 38–40).

38. See Birkland (1997) for a prominent example of this phenomenon—that is, how the 1989 *Exxon Valdez* oil spill created the opportunity for passage of the 1990 Oil Pollution Act.

39. See Rosenbaum (1997, 146–53) for more on this topic.

40. For more on this topic, see Chesapeake Bay Program (1999c, 11).

41. National Commission on the Environment (1993, 8).

42. Also see Rosenbaum (1998, 10–11).

43. See Bosso (1997) and Dunlap, Gallup, and Gallup (1993) for works that track public opinion regarding the environment.

44. See Leach, Pelkey, and Sabatier (2000) for more on collaborative partnerships.

3
SWIMMING AGAINST THE TIDE: NUTRIENT REDUCTION EFFORTS IN THE BAY WATERSHED

1. Horton and Eichbaum (1991, 17–25).

2. See Nixon (1995) for a definition and discussion of *eutrophication*.

3. While there has been debate regarding which nutrient causes the most harm to coastal waters, the general consensus among the scientific community is that nitrogen and phosphorus are the two greatest nutrient threats to the Bay and other coastal waters (National Research Council 2000, 31–36).

4. See "Nutrients: Their Loss Is Bay's Gain, Bay Journal Special Report" (2001).

5. It is important to note that nutrient overenrichment is not a problem unique to the Chesapeake Bay. In a comprehensive study of eutrophication in coastal areas, Bricker et al. (1999) found that 44 of the 138 estuaries they studied showed signs of nutrient overenrichment, with the Mid-Atlantic region and a portion of the Gulf of Mexico experiencing extreme effects. It has been estimated that an area as large as 20,000 square kilometers in the Gulf of Mexico has been damaged by overenrichment (Rabalais et al. 1999). While eutrophication is not unique to the Bay, the Bay's relative shallowness (averaging only 21 feet deep) and the large area of land that drains into the Bay (roughly 64,000 square miles) make the Bay particularly susceptible to the negative effects of eutrophication.

6. The Clean Water Act of 1972 defines *point source pollution* as pollution that can be traced to a single place (i.e., factory, wastewater treatment plant, or other source). Favero (1997) defines *nonpoint source pollution* as "diffused pollution created through surface water runoff and through percolation into the groundwater" (2).

7. The first study that identified hypoxic waters in the Chesapeake Bay was published as early as 1938 (Newcombe and Horne). However, it was not until the early 1980s that scientists began to produce convincing evidence for an increased hypoxia trend in the Bay and to relate the trend to increases in nutrient loading (Taft et al. 1980; Officer et al. 1984). See Boesch, Brinsfield, and Magnien (2001) for a thorough description of anoxia and hypoxia in the Chesapeake Bay.

8. See National Research Council (2000, ch. 1) for more on the general effects of nutrient overenrichment.

9. See Maryland Department of Natural Resources (2000) for a report by the scientific community regarding the link between nutrient overenrichment and *Pfiesteria*. Also see the National Oceanic and Atmospheric Administrations web page www.redtide.whoi.edu/hab for more information regarding harmful algae.

10. Since the initial outbreak in 1997, the Maryland Department of Natural Resources has recorded the presence of *Pfiesteria* in thirteen rivers that feed the Chesapeake Bay, suggesting that *Pfiesteria* has become a widespread problem throughout the region.

11. Associated Press State and Local Wire (2001).

12. See Olin and Kratz (1998) for more on this subject.

13. For more on this topic, see Boesch (1996) and Malone et al. (1993).

14. See Chesapeake Bay Commission (2001b, 17).

15. See Chesapeake Bay Program (1999c, 5) for a description of the importance of nutrient reduction to the Bay Program.

16. Historically, there has been a general trend for populations in the United States to concentrate in coastal regions. While coastal counties comprise only 17 percent of the U.S. landmass, the population in these areas accounts for roughly half the U.S. population (141 million). Moreover, coastal counties account for 17 of the 20 fastest-growing counties in the United States (National Research Council 2000, 14).

17. For more information on this topic, see the Year 2020 Panel Report (1988, 30–31).

18. Swanson (2002).

19. Chesapeake Bay Program (1999c, 25).

20. Chesapeake Bay Program (1999c, 26–27).

21. Chesapeake Bay Program (1997d, 5).

22. See the EPA (1996) for an overview of nutrient management programs dealing with agricultural waste.

23. See Chesapeake Bay Foundation (2000b) for more information on the environmental benefits of smart growth policies.

24. See Maryland Department of Natural Resources (2002b, 11) for cost estimates for nutrient and sediment programs. See Chesapeake Bay Foundation (2001a, 3) and Blankenship (2002b, 2002c) for other works that attempt to estimate the cost of the restoration effort.

25. From Batiuk (2002).

26. A quarter of the nitrogen entering the Bay is estimated to come from the atmospheric pollutants within the airshed (Chesapeake Bay Program 1999c, 32).

27. See Chesapeake Bay Program (1997c, 5) for a description of "uncontrollable" nutrients.

28. Chesapeake Bay Program (1987).

29. Figures from Batiuk (2002).

30. The Chesapeake Bay Program (1999c, 32) estimates that 79 percent of the nitrogen oxide that influences the Bay comes from human activities (i.e., 38 percent from utilities, 35 percent from vehicle emissions, and 6 percent from industry).

31. The most recent version of the model (Phase 4.3) divides the watershed into 94 subsegments and factors in a total of nine land use types. See Linker et al. (2001) for more on the use of modeling by Bay managers.

32. The description of the Bay Program's computer models is based on a March 15, 2002, interview with Richard Batiuk, the associate director for science at the Chesapeake Bay Program and the Linker et al. (2001) publication outlining the history of Chesapeake Bay computer modeling.

33. In this work, the term *validity* describes the extent to which a variable accurately reflects what it is designed to measure. In this case, the chief concept in question is "nutrient loads."

34. Boesch (2002).

35. From Hirshfield (2002). Also see Horton and Eichbaum (1991) for the argument that "accounting procedures almost certainly overstate progress in keeping agricultural nutrients out of the water" (54). Moreover, Boesch (2002) explains that the 1998 status report by the Bay Program serves as a good example of the problems associated with relying on computer models. According to Boesch, within a period of weeks, analysts produced substantially different results, depending on the assumptions that were built into their models.

36. Chesapeake Bay Program (1997c, 1999b, 1999c).

37. From Chesapeake Bay Program (2002d).

38. Significant decreases in total nitrogen were reported at the Patuxent River near Bowie (Maryland) and the Susquehanna River at Towanda (Pennsylvania).

39. Significant increases in total nitrogen were reported at the Patapsco River at Hollofield (Maryland) and North Fork Shenandoah River near Strasburg (Virginia).

40. Significant decreases in total phosphorus were reported at Patuxent River near Bowie (Maryland), James River at Cartersville (Virginia), West Branch Susquehanna River at Lewisburg (Pennsylvania), Georges Creek near Franklin (Maryland), and North Anna River at Hart Corner near Doswell (Virginia).

41. A significant increase in total phosphorus was reported at N F Shenandoah River near Strasburg (Virginia).

42. Environmental Protection Agency (1982).

43. Only the Patapsco River at Hollofield (Maryland) recorded a significant flow increase and a significant increase in total nitrogen.

44. See U.S. Department of the Interior (2001, 13–14) for flow-weighted figures.

45. Karlsen et al. (2000, 505).

46. Sturgis and Murray (1997).

4
THE POLITICAL FIGHT FOR NUTRIENT MANAGEMENT POLICY: THE CASE OF AGRICULTURAL REGULATION

1. See Davison et al. (1997, ch. 8) for an outstanding historical account of sewage management and the Chesapeake Bay.

2. Wolman and Geyer (1962).

3. Davison et al. (1997, 96).

4. See National Research Council (2000, ch. 1) for a general overview of the effects of nutrient overenrichment.

5. See Associated Press State and Local Wire (2002a) and Epstein (2002).

6. See chapter 3 for more on these technologies.

7. Environmental Protection Agency (1983).

8. Favero (1997, 2). Also see Shuyler (1993) and Chesapeake Bay Program (1999c, 24) for more on this topic.

9. Chesapeake Bay Program (1995a, 3). For an estimate that attributes an even larger percent of the Bay's nutrient load to agricultural production, see Chesapeake Bay Program (1988, 3).

10. Chesapeake Bay Program (1995b, 2). Though it is true that agricultural land comprises only 29 percent of all the land in the watershed, it comprises roughly 70 percent of the actively managed land in the watershed (Simpson 2002).

11. Alliance for the Chesapeake Bay (1993, 7–8).

12. "Nutrients: Their Loss Is Bay's Gain, Bay Journal Special Report" (2001, 5–6).

13. The agricultural BMPs considered in the Chesapeake Bay Program analysis were nutrient management, conservation tillage, taking highly erodible lands out of production, structural BMPs, nutrient management, animal waste controls, and pastureland stabilization systems. For a description of each BMP considered, see Chesapeake Bay Program (1995a, 4).

14. The analysis was conducted by the Chesapeake Bay Program at the request of the Chesapeake Bay Commission. Chesapeake Bay Commission (2001b, 35).

15. Chesapeake Bay Program (1997b, 2) estimates that 376 million pounds of nitrogen entered the Bay in 1985, 291 million pounds from nonpoint sources and 85 million from point sources.

16. Chesapeake Bay Program (1995a).

17. Chesapeake Bay Commission (2001b, 35).

18. Calculated by author from "Nutrients: Their Loss Is Bay's Gain, Bay Journal Special Report" (2001, 5).

19. See Chesapeake Bay Commission (1983, 15) for a discussion of Section 208 programs as they relate to the Bay.

20. See Favero (1997) for a state-by-state analysis of nonpoint source nutrient control policies in the Chesapeake Bay states.

21. Maryland was the first to start its cost-sharing programs in 1983. Virginia followed in 1984, and Pennsylvania in 1985.

22. See Chesapeake Bay Commission (1986).

23. In 1991, the year of Governor Schaefer's goal of having Maryland farmers in a critical zone voluntarily adopt management plans, only 42 percent of the farms in the critical area zone had adopted conservation plans. By 2000, neither the 40 percent nitrogen nor the 40 percent phosphorus goals were met.

24. Chesapeake Bay Commission (1986, 31).

25. Select Committee (1990).

26. The Select Committee on Nonpoint Source Nutrients comprised nine members including elected officials, farmers, scientists, and environmentalists. See Select Committee (1990).

27. For a thorough legislative history of Pennsylvania House Bill 100, see Favero (1997, 23–26).

28. Ron Guns no longer chairs the House Environmental Matters Committee and has been replaced by John Hurson, a more Bay-friendly delegate from Montgomery County.

29. The law also established July 1, 2004, as the deadline for farmers to develop phosphorus management plans and to implement them by July 1, 2005.

30. Pennsylvania Farm Bureau (2002).

31. National Agricultural Statistics Service (2002).

32. For more on this study, see Horton and Eichbaum (1991, 51).

33. Chesapeake Bay Program (1995a, 6).

34. Maryland Farm Bureau (2002).

35. In 1998, the family contributed over $25,000 to Maryland candidates.

36. Calculated by author from National Institute on Money in State Politics (2002). Spending figures are from Maryland 1998 elections, Virginia 1999 elections, and Pennsylvania 2000 elections.

37. Maryland State Ethics Commission (2001).

38. Virginia Department of Agriculture (1997).

39. Pennsylvania Farm Bureau (2002).

5
ALL YOU CAN EAT? THE DIFFICULT
TASK OF PROTECTING THE BLUE CRAB

1. For early evidence of the influence of crabs along the Chesapeake, see Davison et al. (1997, 68–69).

2. Dr. John D. Goodman, quoted in Davison et al. (1997, 69).

3. The Chesapeake Bay Program (1997a, 13) estimates that in 1988 alone, Maryland recreational crabbers landed 22 million pounds of crabs.

4. See the Bi-State Blue Crab Advisory Committee (2001b). The survey suggests that commercial fishermen are a fairly homogeneous group: 94 percent are male, 93 percent are Caucasian, and 76 percent are married. Moreover, they represent an aging population, with only 3 percent of Maryland's and 8 percent of Virginia's commercial crabbers under the age of thirty. Conversely, 32 percent of commercial crabbers in Maryland and 27 percent in Virginia are over the age of sixty. Less than 7 percent of licensed crabbers have college degrees.

5. See Horton (1996) for a first-rate account of life in a Chesapeake Bay watermen's community.

6. Baywide from 1981 to 1995, commercial landings of hard crabs averaged 86 million pounds per year. See the Chesapeake Bay Program (1997a) and Bi-State Blue Crab Advisory Committee (2001a, 16).

7. See Maryland Sea Grant (2001).

8. See Chesapeake Bay Commission (1999, 47).

9. The blue crab's Greek name (*Callinectes*) means "beautiful swimmer."

10. This characteristic is also commonly referred to by watermen as "lipstick."

11. See Chesapeake Bay Program (1997a, 7).

12. See Chesapeake Bay Program (1997a, 25).

13. See Law (1996) for information about one of the earliest known blue crab fossils.

14. Beyond harvest totals, the health of the crab population is measured in a number of different ways. Virginia and Maryland conduct annual trawl surveys, which collect crab samples by dragging trawl nets in designated parts of the Bay and its tributaries. Each winter the Chesapeake Bay Winter Dredge Program randomly samples the entire Bay and its tributaries to calculate the health of the stock. Each of these surveys has also shown a general downward trend in the crab population during recent years.

15. See Bi-State Blue Crab Advisory Committee (2001c, 14–15).

16. See Bi-State Blue Crab Advisory Committee (2001c, 15).

17. See Smith, Leffler, and Mackiernan (1992) for an excellent synthesis of the Bay's dissolved oxygen process.

18. Orth et al. (1996).

19. Sindermann (1989), Engel and Noga (1989), and McKenna, Jansen, and Pulley (1990).

20. See Chesapeake Bay Program (1997a, 24) for more on crab diseases.

21. See Casey (1990).

22. Chesapeake Bay Program (1999c, 21). Beyond the damage that mute swans cause to underwater grasses, these massive birds are highly aggressive and threatening to native species. They have been known to kill smaller Canadian geese and other birds that compete with them for nesting spaces. There are even reports of cobs, male swans, aggressively chasing kayakers up to a half mile when protecting a nesting sight.

23. "Ownership" of the Potomac River has long been a source of conflict between Virginia and Maryland. Virginia's claim to the river is based on the fact that the colony's original boundaries included the Potomac River. Maryland, on the other hand, has traditionally argued that it owns the river because King Charles I included the river in the charter he gave to Lord Baltimore in 1632. The Virginia–Maryland Compact of 1785 established that Maryland does in fact own the river, but secured access to its fisheries for Virginia watermen.

24. Bi-State Blue Crab Advisory Committee (2001a).
25. See Chesapeake Bay Program (1989, iv–v) for problem areas and recommended management strategies.
26. See Bi-State Blue Crab Advisory Committee (2001c).

6
BATTLING OVER THE BLUE CRAB: THE POLITICS
OF CRAB MANAGEMENT IN VIRGINIA AND MARYLAND

1. State Game Department of Maryland (1924a, 1924b).
2. Earle (1925).
3. See Virginia Marine Resource Commission (2002) for more on the history of fishery management in Virginia.
4. For an excellent description of the "oyster wars," see Wennersten (1981).
5. For more on the history and function, see the commission's website: www.mrc.state.va.us/.
6. Members of the commission are appointed by the governor and serve renewable, four-year terms.
7. Biographical information from Kale (2002).
8. Coincidently, watermen in more recent times have suggested that the decline in the crab population can be partially attributed to the rebound of the striped bass population, which is believed to feed on juvenile crabs. To date, no scientific studies have made a direct connection between the striped bass's improvement and the crab's decline.
9. See Powell (1967) for more on the history of fisheries management in Maryland.
10. While Virginia also has a cabinet-level position that addresses environmental issues, the Department of Conservation and Recreation, this agency is not in charge of marine resources in the state.
11. See McKee (1970) for more on the 1969 reform of natural resource management in Maryland.
12. The current director of fisheries services is Eric Schwaab, who was appointed by the secretary of natural resources in 1999 after serving in various capacities with the Department of Natural Resources since 1983.
13. Governor Glendening has a well-earned reputation for maintaining firm control over the Department of Natural Resources. Between 1995 and 2002, Glendening was involved in minute details of the department's regulatory actions. His willingness to remove heads of the agency, three during his administration (Torrey Brown, John Griffin, and Sara Taylor-Rogers), helped maintain his influence over the agency.
14. From 2002 interview with Stuart Buppert (assistant attorney general at Maryland Department of Natural Resources).

15. Baywide from 1981 to 1995, commercial landings of hard crabs averaged 86 million pounds per year. See the Chesapeake Bay Program (1997a) and Bi-State Blue Crab Advisory Committee (2001a, 16).

16. Maryland Sea Grant (2001).

17. Lipton and Sullivan (2002).

18. See Bi-State Blue Crab Advisory Committee (2001b, 11) for more on the cost of commercial crabbing.

19. Bi-State Blue Crab Advisory Committee (2001b, 4).

20. See Simns (2001) for a description of the conflict.

21. National Institute on Money in State Politics (2002).

22. For more on Simns, see Burton (2001).

23. The Virginia watermen's associations including Saxis Watermen's Association, Working Watermen's Association, Eastern Shore Watermen's Association, Tangier Watermen's Association, Lower Chesapeake Bay Watermen's Association, Lower Eastern Shore Watermen's Association, Hampton Roads Watermen's Association, Upper River Watermen's Association, and York River/Croaker Landing Working Watermen's Association.

24. See Collins (2000) for an excellent discussion of the tragedy of the commons and the Chesapeake Bay's blue crab fishery.

25. The totals were calculated by the author from a search of the Lexis-Nexis, Academic Universe, U.S. News database for the two states, using the search term "blue crab." The Lexis-Nexis newspaper database for Maryland and Virginia papers is incomplete for dates prior to 1994.

7
TOWARD A BRIGHTER FUTURE FOR THE CHESAPEAKE BAY

1. See Davison et al. (1997, ch.13) for more on the history Bay bureaucracy.

2. See Section 303(d) of the federal Clean Water Act (CWA, 33 USC 1250, et seq., at 1313[d]).

3. Horton (1999).

4. Chesapeake Bay Commission (1981, A-3).

5. See chapter 1 of this work for a description of federally funded programs for the Bay.

6. For example, a promising Nutrient Reduction Pilot Program that would have provided farmers with economic incentives to limit fertilizer use and would have substantially reduced the Bay's nutrient load was cut from the most recent Farm Bill.

7. The composition of the 64,000-square-mile watershed is as follows: Delaware (1 percent), District of Columbia (0.1 percent), Maryland (14 percent), New York (10 percent), Pennsylvania (35 percent), Virginia (34 percent), and West Virginia (6 percent).

8. See Sabato, Ernst, and Larson (2001) for more on the arguments for and against ballot initiatives.

9. Myers (1999, 2001).

10. Trust for Public Land (2002).

11. Maryland allows for citizens to challenge laws after they have been passed by the General Assembly but has no mechanism for citizens to propose legislation.

12. Ballot Watch (2002b).

13. For more information on the Sierra Club's political activity, see Mundo (1992, ch. 7).

14. From Denise Stranko (2002).

15. Sue Brown directs the Maryland League of Conservation Voters. Brown worked at the Chesapeake Bay Foundation for five years as a grassroots coordinator before leaving to take her current position at the league.

16. For example, see Truman (1951), Cobb and Elder (1983), Kingdon (1984), and Birkland (1997).

17. Maryland, Virginia, and Pennsylvania are currently attempting to estimate the cost of meeting the goals of the 2000 Chesapeake Bay Agreement. See Blankenship (2002b) for an analysis that put the cost of restoration at roughly $20 billion.

18. Blankenship (2002d).

19. Horton (2002b).

References

Alliance for the Chesapeake Bay. 1993. "Nutrients and the Chesapeake: Refining the Bay Cleanup Effort." White paper. Baltimore: Alliance for the Chesapeake Bay.

Anderson, James. 1975. *Public Policy-Making.* New York: Praeger.

Anderson, Terry L., and Peter J. Hill, eds. 1997. *Environmental Federalism.* Lanham, Md.: Rowman & Littlefield.

Associated Press State and Local Wire. 2001. "Scientists Find Harmful Algae in Chesapeake Bay." Annapolis, Md., July 9.

———. 2002a. "Hagerstown Sewage Plant Nearly Back to Normal." Hagerstown, Md., February 19.

———. 2002b. "Hatchery Crab Release Planned to Try to Boost Dwindling Wild Population." *Bay Journal* 12, no. 2 (June 17), at www.bayjournal.com/02-04/crab.htm (accessed November 1, 2002).

Ayres, Robert U., and Allen V. Kneese. 1969. "Production, Consumption, and Externalities." *American Economic Review* LIX (June): 282–97.

Bacot, A. Hunter, and Roy A. Dawes. 1997. "State Expenditures and Policy Outcomes in Environmental Management." *Policy Studies Journal* 25, no. 2: 355–70.

Ballot Watch. 2002a. *Maryland,* at www.iandrinstitute.org/asp/history.asp?state=Maryland&frm_from=ballotwatch (accessed June 14, 2002).

———. 2002b. *Virginia,* at www.iandrinstitute.org/asp/history.asp?state=Virginia&frm_from=ballotwatch (accessed June 14, 2002).

Batiuk, Richard. 2002. Interview by author. Annapolis, Md., March 15.

Baumgartner, Frank R., and Bryan D. Jones. 1993. *Agendas and Instability in American Politics.* Chicago: University of Chicago Press.

Beatty, R. C., and W. J. Mulloy. 1940. *William Byrd's Natural History of Virginia or the Newly Discovered Eden.* Richmond, Va.: Dietz Press.

Belval, Donna L., and Lori A. Sprague. 1999. "Monitoring Nutrients in the Major Rivers Draining to Chesapeake Bay." *U.S. Geological Survey, Water-Resources Investigations Report,* at va.water.usgs.gov/online_pubs/WRIR/99-4238/99-4238.html (accessed June 19, 2002).

Birkland, Thomas A. 1997. *After the Disaster: Agenda Setting, Public Policy, and Focusing Events.* Washington, D.C.: Georgetown University Press.

Bi-State Blue Crab Advisory Committee. 2001a. *The Chesapeake Bay Blue Crab: Harvest Trends and Dockside Values.* Annapolis, Md.: Chesapeake Bay Commission.

———. 2001b. *The Chesapeake Bay Commercial Blue Crab Fishery: A Socio-Economic Profile.* Annapolis, Md.: Chesapeake Bay Commission.

———. 2001c. *Taking Action for the Blue Crab: Managing and Protecting the Stock and Its Fisheries.* Annapolis, Md.: Chesapeake Bay Commission.

Blankenship, Karl. 2001a. "Bay Program Unveils Draft Criteria for Clean Bay." *Bay Journal* 11, no. 5, at www.bayjournal.com/01-07/criteria.htm#do (accessed June 21, 2002).

———. 2001b. "Past Political Leaders Reflect on Restoration Efforts' Past, Future." *Bay Journal* 11, no. 3, at www.bayjournal.com/01-05/dialogue.htm (accessed June 17, 2002).

———. 2002a. "Bill Would Offer Federal Aid to Wastewater Plants." *Bay Journal* 12, no. 4, at www.bayjournal.com/02-06/bnr.htm (accessed June 17 2002).

———. 2002b. "Maryland Tab for Bay Goals put at $7 Billion." *Bay Journal* 11, no. 10, at www.bayjournal.com/02-01/mdcost.htm (accessed June 17, 2002).

———. 2002c. "VA Comes Up with Cost for Cleanup; Now It Must Come Up with Money." *Bay Journal* 12, no.1, at www.bayjournal.com/02-03/va.htm (accessed June 17, 2002).

———. 2002d. "VA Seafood Council Postpones Plans for *Ariakensis* Project." *Bay Journal* 12, no. 4, at www.bayjounral.com/02-06/oysters.htm (accessed June 17, 2002).

Boesch, Donald F. 1996. "Science and Management in Four U.S. Coastal Ecosystems Dominated by Land–Ocean Interactions." *Journal of Coastal Conservation* 2: 103–14.

———. 2002. Interview by author. Annapolis, Md., March 22, 2002.

Boesch, Donald F., Russell B. Brinsfield, and Robert E. Magnien. 2001. "Chesapeake Bay Eutrophication: Scientific Understanding, Ecosystem Restoration, and Challenges for Agriculture." *Journal of Environmental Quality* 30: 303–20.

Bosso, Christopher J. 1997. "Seizing Back the Day: The Challenge of Environmental Activism in the 1990s." In *Environmental Policy in the 1990's: Reform or Reaction,* 3d ed., ed. Norman J. Vig and Michael E. Kraft, pp. 53–75. Washington, D.C.: Congressional Quarterly Press.

Bricker, S. B., C. G. Clement, D. E. Pirhalla, S. P. Orlando, and D. G. Farrow. 1999. *National Estuarine Eutrophication Assessment: Effects of Nutrient Enrichment in the Nation's Estuaries.* Silver Spring, Md.: National Oceanic and Atmospheric Administration.

Buppert, Stuart G. 2002. Interview by author. Annapolis, Md., May 31.

Burton, Bill. 2001. "Watermen Leader Larry Simns: He Knows How to Play the Game." *Waterman's Gazette* (September): 13.

Caldwell, Lynton K. 1963. "Environment: A New Focus for Public Policy?" *Public Administration Review* 23: 132–39.

Campbell, James E., and James C. Garand, eds. 2000. *Before the Vote: Forecasting American National Elections.* Thousand Oaks, Calif.: Sage.

Carson, Rachel. 1962. *Silent Spring.* Boston: Houghton Mifflin.

Casey, J. 1990. *A Study of Biodegradable Escape Panels in Crab Pots.* Annapolis, Md.: Maryland Department of Natural Resources Tidal Fisheries Division.

Castillo, Eloise Trabka, Mark L. Morris, and Robert S. Raucher. 1997. "Great Lakes Water Quality Guidance." In *Economic Analysis at the EPA: Assessing Regulatory Impact,* ed. Richard D. Morgenstern, pp. 419–55. Washington D.C.: Resources for the Future.

Center for American Politics and Citizenship. 1999. "Contributions to Maryland General Assembly Candidates in the 1998 Elections." College Park, Md.: University of Maryland's Center for American Politics and Citizenship, at www.capc.umd.edu/rpts/MDGA98.CONT.pdf (accessed June 6, 2002).

Chesapeake Bay Authority. 1933. *Chesapeake Bay Authority.* Conference proceedings from the Chesapeake Bay Authority meeting, October 6, Baltimore, Md.

Chesapeake Bay Commission. 1981. *Annual Report: 1980–1981.* Annapolis, Md.: Chesapeake Bay Commission.

———. 1983. *Annual Report to the General Assemblies of Maryland and Virginia: 1983.* Annapolis, Md.: Chesapeake Bay Commission.

———. 1985. *Annual Report to the General Assemblies of Maryland, Pennsylvania, and Virginia: 1985.* Annapolis, Md.: Chesapeake Bay Commission.

———. 1986. *Annual Report to the General Assemblies of Pennsylvania, Maryland, and Virginia: 1986.* Annapolis, Md.: Chesapeake Bay Commission.

———. 1994. *Annual Report 1994: Policy for the Bay.* Annapolis, Md.: Chesapeake Bay Commission.

———. 1999. *Annual Report to the General Assemblies of Virginia, Maryland, and Pennsylvania: 1999.* Annapolis, Md.: Chesapeake Bay Commission.

———. 2000. *Special Report.* Annapolis, Md.: Chesapeake Bay Commission.

———. 2001a. *Legislative Update.* Annapolis, Md.: Chesapeake Bay Commission.

———. 2001b. *Seeking Solutions: Chesapeake Bay Commission, Annual Report.* Annapolis, Md.: Chesapeake Bay Commission.

Chesapeake Bay Foundation. 1998. *Save the Bay.* Annapolis, Md.: Chesapeake Bay Foundation.

———. 2000a. *2000 Annual Report.* Annapolis, Md.: Chesapeake Bay Foundation.

———. 2000b. *Land and the Chesapeake Bay.* Annapolis, Md.: Chesapeake Bay Foundation.

———. 2000c. *The State of the Bay Report 2000.* Annapolis, Md.: Chesapeake Bay Foundation.

———. 2001a. "$8.5 Billion: The Price of a Saved Bay." *Chesapeake Bay Foundation Save the Bay Quarterly Newsletter* 27, no. 2: 3.

———. 2001b. "General Information about the Bay," at www.cbf.org/resources/facts/general.htm (accessed June 6, 2002).

———. 2002a. "Poor Water Quality Inhibits Chesapeake Bay Improvements in 2001." *Save the Bay,* at cbf.org/sotb/index.htm (accessed June 20, 2002).

———. 2002b. "Toxic Chemicals Taint Fish in Most MD Rivers," at www.cbf.org/resources/news_room/nb/2001/nb_2001_12_13.htm (accessed June 14, 2002).

Chesapeake Bay Non-Point Source Panel. 1990. *The Chesapeake Bay Nonpoint Source Program Evaluation Panel.* Final report. Annapolis, Md.: Chesapeake Bay Program.

Chesapeake Bay Program. 1987. *1987 Chesapeake Bay Agreement.* Annapolis, Md.: Chesapeake Bay Program.

———. 1988. *Chesapeake Bay Nonpoint Source Programs.* Annapolis, Md.: Environmental Protection Agency.

———. 1989. *Chesapeake Bay Blue Crab Management Plan.* Annapolis, Md.: Environmental Protection Agency.

———. 1994. *Achieving the Chesapeake Bay Nutrient Goals.* Annapolis, Md.: Environmental Protection Agency.

———. 1995a. *Cost Analysis for Nonpoint Source Control Strategies in the Chesapeake Basin.* Annapolis, Md.: Environmental Protection Agency.

———. 1995b. *The State of the Bay 1995.* Annapolis, Md.: Environmental Protection Agency.

———. 1997a. *1997 Chesapeake Bay Blue Crab Fishery Management Plan.* Annapolis, Md.: Environmental Protection Agency.

———. 1997b. *Analyzing Nonpoint Source Water Pollution Problems: Nutrient Control Policies in the Chesapeake Bay State.* Annapolis, Md.: Environmental Protection Agency.

———. 1997c. *Chesapeake Bay: Nutrient Reduction Progress and Future Directions.* Annapolis, Md.: Environmental Protection Agency.

———. 1997d. *The Potential for Nutrient Loadings from Septic Systems to Ground and Surface Water Resources and the Chesapeake Bay.* Annapolis, Md.: Environmental Protection Agency.

———. 1999a. *Chesapeake Bay Living Resources 1998.* Annapolis, Md.: Environmental Protection Agency.

———. 1999b. *Snapshot of the Chesapeake Bay: How Is It Doing?* Fact sheet. Annapolis, Md.: Chesapeake Bay Program.

———. 1999c. *The State of the Bay: A Report to the Citizens of the Bay Region.* Annapolis, Md.: Environmental Protection Agency.

———. 2000. *Chesapeake Bay: How Is It Doing?* Fact sheet. Annapolis, Md.: Chesapeake Bay Program.

———. 2002a. "Blue Crab Life Stages." *Blue Crab,* at www.chesapeakebay.net/baybio.htm (accessed June 21, 2002).

———. 2002b. "Chesapeake Bay Program Organizational Structure." *Committee Activities Information,* at www.chesapeakebay.net/committee.htm (accessed November 1, 2002).

———. 2002c. "Chesapeake Bay Watershed Organizations," at www.chesapeakebay.net/wshed_directory.htm (accessed June 21, 2002).

———. 2002d. *The State of the Bay: A Report to the Citizens of the Bay Region.* Annapolis, Md.: Environmental Protection Agency.

———. 2002e. "Watershed Profiles," at www.chesapeakebay.net/wshed.htm (accessed June 21, 2002).

Cobb, Roger W., and Charles D. Elder. 1983. *Participation in American Politics: The Dynamics of Agenda-Building.* 2d ed. Baltimore: Johns Hopkins University Press.

Collins, Richard C. 2000. *The Commons Trap and Fishery Deliberations.* Charlottesville: Virginia Sea Grant.

Commoner, Barry. 1971. *The Closing Circle.* New York: Knopf.

Connelly, James, and Graham Smith. 1999. *Politics and the Environment: From Theory to Practice.* New York: Routledge.

Conservation Department of Maryland. 1923. *The First Annual Report of the Conservation Department of the State of Maryland.* Baltimore: Conservation Department of Maryland.

Cooper, S. R. 1995. "Chesapeake Bay Watershed Historical Land Use: Impact on Water Quality and Diatom Communities." *Ecology* 5: 703–23.

Cooper, S. R., and G. S. Brush. 1991. "Long-Term History of Chesapeake Bay Anoxia." *Science* 254: 992–96.

Coyle, David Cushan. 1957. *Conservation.* New Brunswick, N.J.: Rutgers University Press.

Crenson, Matthew. 1971. *The Un-Politics of Air Pollution: A Study of Non-Decisionmaking in the Cities.* Baltimore: Johns Hopkins University Press.

Crooks, James B. 1968. *Politics and Progress: The Rise of Urban Progressivism in Baltimore 1895–1911.* Baton Rouge: Louisiana State University Press.

Curtin, Philip D., Grace S. Brush, and George W. Fisher, eds. 2001. *Discovering the Chesapeake: The History of an Ecosystem.* Baltimore: Johns Hopkins University Press.

Davies, J. Clarence, and Jan Mazurek. 1997. *Regulating Pollution: Does the U.S. System Work?* Washington, D.C.: Resources for the Future.

Davis, Charles. 1992. "State Environmental Regulation and Economic Development: Are They Compatible?" *Policy Studies Review* 11, no. 2: 149–57.

Davison, Steve G., Jay G. Merwin Jr., John Capper, Garrett Power, and Frank R. Shivers Jr. 1997. *Chesapeake Waters: Four Centuries of Controversy, Concern, and Legislation.* Centreville, Md.: Tidewater.

Dennison, W., R. Orth, K. Moore, J. Stevenson, V. Carter, S. Kollar, P. Bergstrom, and R. Batiuk. 1993. "Assessing Water Quality with Submerged Aquatic Vegetation." *BioScience* 43, no. 2: 86–94.

Dobson, Andrew, ed. 1991. *The Green Reader: Essays toward a Sustainable Society.* San Francisco: Mercury House.

Downs, Anthony. 1972. "Up and Down with Ecology: The 'Issue-Attention Cycle.'" *Public Interest* 28 (summer): 38–50.

Duerksen, Christopher J. 1983. *Environmental Regulation of Industrial Plant Siting: How to Make It Work Better.* Washington D.C.: Conservation Foundation.

Dunlap, Riley E., George H. Gallup, and Alec M. Gallup. 1993. "Of Global Concern: Results of the Health of the Planet Survey." *Environment* 35, no. 9: 33–40.

Earle, Swepson. 1925. "Crab Conservation." *Maryland Conservationist* (summer): 18.

Ehrlich, Paul R. 1968. *The Population Bomb.* New York: Ballantine.

Eisinger, Peter K. 1988. *The Rise of the Entrepreneurial State: States and Local Economic Development Policy in the United States.* Madison: University of Wisconsin Press.

Emerson, Ralph Waldo. [1836] 1982. "Nature." Reprint in *Ralph Waldo Emerson: Selected Essays,* ed. Larzer Ziff. New York: Penguin.

———. [1876] 1903. "Politics." Reprint in *Essays by Ralph Waldo Emerson,* Second Series. Boston: Houghton, Mifflin.

Engel, D., and E. Noga. 1989. "Shell Disease in the Blue Crabs of the Pamlico River." *Environs* (February): 3–5.

Engel, Kirsten H. 1997. "State Environmental Standard Setting: Is There a 'Race to the Bottom'?" *Hastings Law Journal* 48, no. 2: 271–398.

Environmental Protection Agency (EPA). 1982. *Chesapeake Bay: A Profile of Environmental Change.* Washington, D.C.: Environmental Protection Agency.

———. 1983. *A Framework for Action.* Philadelphia: Environmental Protection Agency.

———. 1988a. *Chesapeake Bay Nonpoint Source Programs.* Annapolis, Md.: Chesapeake Bay Liaison Office.

———. 1988b. *Point Source Atlas.* Washington, D.C.: Environmental Protection Agency.

———. 1992. "The Guardian: Origins of the EPA." *EPA History,* at www.epa.gov/history/publications/origins.htm (accessed June 6, 2002).

———. 1996. *Chesapeake Bay Area Nutrient Management Programs*. Washington, D.C.: Environmental Protection Agency.

———. 1997. *Mid-Atlantic States: State of the Environment*. Washington, D.C.: Environmental Protection Agency.

———. 1998. *The Regional NO$_x$ SIP Call and Reduced Atmospheric Deposition of Nitrogen: Benefits to Selected Estuaries*. Washington, D.C.: Environmental Protection Agency.

———. 2000. *Chesapeake Bay: Introduction to an Ecosystem*. Washington, D.C.: Environmental Protection Agency.

Epstein, Gady A. 2002. "Aging Sewers May Cost City $900 Million." *Baltimore Sun*, February 9.

Erickson, Robert S. 1989. "Economic Conditions and the Presidential Vote." *American Political Science Review* 83 (June): 567–73.

Favero, Phillip. 1997. *Analyzing Nonpoint Source Water Pollution Problems: Nutrient Control Policies in the Chesapeake Bay States*. Annapolis, Md.: Environmental Protection Agency.

Feiock, Richard, and C. K. Rowland. 1991. "Environmental Regulation and Economic Development." *Western Political Quarterly* 44, no. 2: 561–76.

Feiock, Richard, and Christopher Stream. 2001. "Environmental Protection versus Economic Development: A False Trade-Off?" *Public Administration Review* 61 (May/June): 313–21.

Feldman, Stanley. 1982. "Economic Self-interest and Political Behavior." *American Journal of Political Science* 26: 446–66.

Fisher, George W., and Jerry R. Schubel. 2001. "The Chesapeake Ecosystem: Its Geological Heritage." In *Discovering the Chesapeake: The History of an Ecosystem*, ed. Philip D. Curtin, Grace S. Brush, and George W. Fisher. Baltimore: Johns Hopkins University Press.

Fowler, Bernie. 2001. Comment made at a "Dialogue" sponsored by the Alliance for the Chesapeake Bay, the Bay Program, and the Washington College Center for Environment and Society, in which past elected officials discussed the Bay restoration, April 7.

Freeman, A. Myrick, III, and Robert H. Havenam. 1972. "Clean Rhetoric, Dirty Water." *Public Interest* 28 (Summer): 51–65.

Furlong, Scott R. 1997. "Interest Group Influence on Rulemaking." *Administration and Society* 29 (July): 325–47.

Graham, Otis L., Jr., ed. 2000. *Environmental Politics and Policy, 1960–1990s*. University Park: Pennsylvania State University Press.

Grattan, Lynn M., David Oldach, Trish M. Perl, Mark H. Lowitt, Diane L. Matuszak, Curtis Dickson, Colleen Parrott, Ritchie C. Shoemaker, C. Lisa Kauffman, Martin P. Wasserman, J Richard Hebel, Patricia Charache, and J. Glenn Morris Jr. 1998. "Learning and Memory Difficulties after Environmental Exposure to Waterways Containing Toxin-Producing *Pfiesteria* or *Pfiesteria*-Like Dinoflagellates." *Lancet*: 532–39.

Greer, Jack. 2002. E-mail correspondence with author, August 8.

Hardin, Garrett. 1968. "The Tragedy of the Commons." *Science* 162: 1243–48.

Hibbs, Douglas A., Jr. 1987. *The American Political Economy.* Cambridge, Mass.: Harvard University Press.

Hirshfield, Mike. 2002. Telephone interview by author, March 29.

Hofferbert, Richard. 1974. *The Study of Public Policy.* Indianapolis: Bobbs-Merrill.

Horton, Tom. 1996. *An Island Out of Time: A Memoir of Smith Island in the Chesapeake.* New York: W. W. Norton.

———. 1999. "Agency's 'Fish-Eye' View: TMDL: The EPA Proposes to Create Enforceable Overall Limits on Water Pollutants, Giving Teeth to the Cleanup Effort." *Baltimore Sun,* August 20, p. 2B.

———. 2001. "Cherishing the Chesapeake." *Land and People: The Trust for Public Land (Annual Report)* 13, no. 2: 3–9.

———. 2002a. "Costs to Conserve Pale Next to Costs of Collapse." *Baltimore Sun,* May 24, p. 2B.

———. 2002b. Interview by author. Annapolis, Md., February 28.

Horton, Tom, and William M. Eichbaum. 1991. *Turning the Tide: Saving the Chesapeake Bay.* Washington, D.C.: Island Press.

Hughes, Harry. 2002. Interview by author. Denton, Md., April 5.

Hylander, Tim. 2001. "Recent Weather Killing Fish: Thousands Suffocate Due to Heat and Lack of Breeze." *Capital,* July 7, p. 2A.

Jones, Charles. 1970. *An Introduction to the Study of Public Policy.* Belmont, Calif.: Wadsworth.

Jones, Holway R. 1965. *John Muir and the Sierra Club: The Battle for Yosemite.* San Francisco: Sierra Club.

Kale, Wilford. 2002. Telephone interview by author, May 30.

Karlsen, A. W., T. M. Cronin, S. E. Ishman, D. A. Willard, R. Kerhin, C. W. Holmes, and M. Marot. 2000. "Historical Trend in the Chesapeake Bay Dissolved Oxygen Based on Bethic Foraminifera from Sediment Cores." *Estuaries* 23, no. 4: 488–508.

Kinder, Donald R., and D. Roderick Kiewiet. 1979. "Economic Discontent and Political Behavior: The Role of Personal Grievances and Collective Economic Judgments in Congressional Voting." *American Journal of Political Science* 23: 495–527.

Kingdon, John. 1984. *Agendas, Alternatives, and Public Policies.* Boston: Little, Brown.

Kirkley, James, William DuPaul, and Michael Oesterling. 1995. *Regulating the Blue Crab, Callinectes Sapidus, Fishery in Virginia: Biological and Economic Concerns.* Gloucester Point: Virginia Institute of Marine Science.

Kiser, Larry, and Elinor Ostrom. 1982. "The Three Worlds of Action." In *Strategies of Political Inquiry,* ed. Elinor Osrom. Beverly Hills: Sage.

Kraft, Michael E. 2001. *Environmental Policy and Politics.* New York: Addison-Wesley.

Law, Daryl L. 1996. "Corolla Crab Is an Oldster." *Outer Banks Sentinel,* at www.blue-crab.org/fossil.htm (accessed June 5, 2002).

Leach, William D., Neil W. Pelkey, and Paul A Sabatier. 2000. "Conceptualizing and Measuring Success in Collaborative Watershed Partnerships." Paper presented at the annual meeting of the American Political Science Association, Washington, D.C.

Leopold, Aldo. [1913] 1991. "To the Forrest Officers of the Carson." In *The River of the Mother of God,* ed. Susan Flader and J. Baird Callicott. Madison: University of Wisconsin Press.

——. 1949. *The Sand County Almanac.* New York: Oxford University Press.

Lester, James P. 1994. "A New Federalism? Environmental Policy in the States." In *Environmental Policy in the 1990s: Toward a New Agenda,* 2d ed., ed. Norman Vig and Michael E. Kraft, pp. 51–69. Washington D.C.: Congressional Quarterly Press.

Lewis-Beck, Michael S., and Tom W. Rice. 1992. *Forecasting Elections.* Washington, D.C.: Congressional Quarterly Press.

Lindstrom, Matthew J., and Zachary A. Smith. 2001. *The National Environmental Policy Act: Judicial Misconstruction, Legislative Indifference, and Executive Neglect.* College Station: Texas A & M University Press.

Linker, Lewis C., Gary W. Shenk, Ping Wang, Katherine J. Hopkins, Sajan Pokharel. 2001. *A Short History of Chesapeake Bay Modeling and the Next Generation of Watershed and Estuarine Models.* Annapolis, Md.: Chesapeake Bay Commission.

Lipton, Douglas. 2002. Telephone interview by author, May 28.

Lipton, Douglas, and Shannon Sullivan. 2002. "The Economic Impact on Maryland's Crabmeat Processing Industry of Proposed Regulations: A Possession Restriction on Sponge Crabs and Crabs Smaller than 5¼ Inches." *Maryland Sea Grant Extension Program Publication,* at www.mdsg.umd.edu/crabs/econ_rpt/index.html (accessed June 8, 2002).

Lynch, James F. 2001. "Bird Populations of the Chesapeake Bay Region: 350 Years of Change." In *Discovering the Chesapeake: The History of an Ecosystem,* ed. Philip D. Curtin, Grace S. Brush, and George W. Fisher, pp. 322–55. Baltimore: Johns Hopkins University Press.

Malone, T. C., W. Boyton, T. Horton, and C. Stevenson. 1993. "Nutrient Loading to Surface Waters: Chesapeake Bay Case Study." In *Keeping Pace with Science and Engineering,* ed. M. F. Uman, pp. 8–38. Washington D.C.: National Academy Press.

Marsh, George Perkins. 1864. *Man and Nature.* New York: Scribner.

Martin, Paul S., and R. G. Klein, eds. 1984. *Quaternary Extinctions.* Tucson: University of Arizona Press.

Marx, Peter J. 1999. "Rhinos and Tigers and Bays (Oh My!), and Other Congressional Tales." *George Wright Forum* 16: 39–44.

Maryland Department of the Environment. 1999. "Overall Nitrogen Sources to the Bay." *Maryland's Environmental Indicators,* at www.mde.state.md.us/enpa/2000_enpa/envi_indicators/wq_eco/graphics/e61_gr.htm (accessed June 21, 2002).

Maryland Department of Natural Resources. 2000. "*Pfiesteria* and Fish Health: Summary of Phiesteria Investigations in Maryland." *Pfiesteria Information,* at www.dnr.state.md.us/pfiesteria/sop.html (accessed June 5, 2002).

———. 2001. "What You Should Know about *Pfiesteria Piscicida.*" *Pfiesteria Information,* at www.dnr.state.md.us/pfiesteria/facts.html (accessed June 5, 2002).

———. 2002a. "Baywide Bay Grass Coverage." *Chesapeake Bay,* at www.dnr.state.md.us/bay/sav/coverage_habitat.html (accessed November 1, 2002).

———. 2002b. *Financial Analysis for the Restoration of the Chesapeake Bay in Maryland.* Annapolis: Maryland Department of Natural Resources.

Maryland Farm Bureau. 2002. "Nutrient Management Update (January 31, 2002)." *Nutrient Planning,* at www.mdfarmbureau.com/NMIupdatepage.htm (accessed June 5, 2002).

Maryland Nutrient Cap Workgroup. 2001. "Maryland's Interim Nutrient Cap Strategy." *Nutrient Planning,* at www.dnr.state.md.us/tribstrat/index.html (accessed June 5, 2002).

Maryland Sea Grant. 2001. *Research Needs for Sustainable Blue Crab Production in Maryland.* College Park: Maryland Sea Grant College.

Maryland State Ethics Commission. 2001. "Twenty-Second Annual Report (January 1, 2000–December 31, 2000)," at ethics.gov.state.md.us/report.htm#Lobbyist_Expenditures (accessed June 8, 2002).

McCloskey, Michael. 1992. "Twenty Years of Change in the Environmental Movement: An Insider's View." In *American Environmentalism: The U.S. Environmental Movement, 1970–1990,* ed. Riley E. Dunlap and Angela G. Mertig. Philadelphia: Traylor and Francis.

McKee, Paul W. 1970. "State Government Reorganization in the Field of Ecology and Environment: An Example from the East." *Maryland Conservationist* (December): 4–7.

McKenna, S., M. Jansen, and M. Pulley. 1990. "Shell Disease of the Blue Crabs, *Callinectes Sapidus,* in the Pamlico River, North Carolina." North Carolina Division of Marine Fisheries Special Scientific Report no. 51.

Mencken, H. L. 1940. *Happy Days.* New York: Knopf.

Miller, Norman. 2001. *Environmental Politics: Interest Groups, the Media, and the Making of Policy.* Boca Raton, Fla.: Lewis.

Millhouser, W. C., J. McDonough, J. P. Tolson, and D. Slade. 1998. *Managing Coastal Resources.* Silver Spring, Md.: National Oceanic and Atmospheric Administration.

Moe, Terry. 1984. "The New Economics of Organization," *American Journal of Political Science* 28 (November): 739–77.

Morgenstern, Richard D., ed. 1997. *Economic Analysis at the EPA: Assessing Regulatory Impact.* Washington D.C.: Resources for the Future.

Muir, John. 1894. *The Mountains of California.* New York: Century.

Mundo, Philip A. 1992. *Interest Groups: Cases and Characteristics.* Chicago: Nelson-Hall.

Myers, Phyllis. 1999. "Livability at the Ballot Box: State and Local Referenda on Parks, Conservation, and Smart Growth, Election Day 1998." Discussion paper. Washington, D.C.: Brookings Institution.

———. 2001. "Growth at the Ballot Box: Electing the Shape of Communities in November 2000." Discussion paper. Washington, D.C.: Brookings Institution.

Nash, Roderick. 1974. *The Conservation Movement.* St. Charles, Mo.: Forum.

———. 1982. *Wilderness and the American Mind.* New Haven, Conn.: Yale University Press.

———. 1988. *The Rights of Nature: A History of Environmental Ethics.* Madison: University of Wisconsin Press.

———. 1990. *American Environmentalism.* 3d ed. New York: McGraw-Hill.

National Agricultural Statistics Service. 2002. "State Offices." *State Offices Information,* at www.usda.gov/nass/sso-rpts.htm (accessed June 5, 2002).

National Commission on the Environment. 1993. *Choosing a Sustainable Future.* Washington, D.C.: Island Press.

National Institute on Money in State Politics. 2002. "1998 Maryland Data Base." *Campaign Finance,* at www.followthemoney.org/database/stateview.phtml?s=MD (accessed June 5, 2002).

National Marine Fisheries Service. 2001. "Annual Commercial Landing Statistics." *Commercial Fisheries,* at www.st.nmfs.gov/commercial/landings/annual_landings.html (accessed June 20, 2002).

National Oceanic and Atmospheric Administration (NOAA). 1998. "Chesapeake Bay Water Quality Analysis: Dissolved Oxygen July 1998." *Image Gallery,* at noaa.chesapeakebay.net/data/interp1.htm (accessed June 21, 2002).

———. 2001. "2001 Chesapeake Bay Blue Crab Advisory Report." *Chesapeake Bay Report,* at noaa.chesapeakebay.net/reports/BCARpage2001.htm (accessed June 5, 2002).

———. 2002. "NOAA Chesapeake Bay Office." *General Information,* at noaa.chesapeakebay.net (accessed June 5, 2002).

National Research Council. 2000. *Clean Coastal Waters: Understanding and Reducing the Effects of Nutrient Pollution.* Washington, D.C.: National Academy Press.

Newcombe, C. L., and W. A. Horne. 1938. "Oxygen Poor Waters in the Chesapeake Bay. *Science* 88: 80.

Newell, R. I. E. 1988. "Ecological Changes in Chesapeake Bay: Are They the Result of Over Harvesting the American Oyster, *Crassotrea virginica*?" In *Understanding the Estuary: Advances in Chesapeake Bay Research.* Baltimore: Chesapeake Bay Consortium Publication 129: 536–46.

Nixon, S. W. 1995. "Coastal Marine Eutrophication: A Definition, Social Causes, and Future Concerns." *Ophelia* 41: 199–219.

"Nutrients: Their Loss Is Bay's Gain, Bay Journal Special Report." 2001. *Bay Journal* 10, no. 10, at www.bayjournal.com/01-01/index.htm (accessed June 17, 2002).

Oates, Wallace E., ed. 1992. *The Economics of the Environment.* Cambridge: Cambridge University Press.

Officer, C. B., R. B. Biggs, J. L. Taft, L. E. Cronin, M. A. Tyler, and W. R. Boynton. 1984. "Chesapeake Bay Anoxia: Origin, Development, and Significance." *Science* 223: 22–27.

Olin, Dirk, and Vikki Kratz. 1998. "Chicken Sick." *Mother Jones* (July/August), at www.motherjones.com/mother_jones/JA98/chicken.html (accessed November 1, 2002).

Olson, Mancur, Jr. 1965. *The Logic of Collective Action: Public Goods and the Theory of Goods.* Cambridge, Mass.: Harvard University Press.

Orth, R. J., J. van Montfrans, R. N. Lipcius, and K. S. Metcalf. 1996. "Utilization of Seagrass Habitat by the Blue Crab." In *Seagrass Biology: Proceeds of the International Workshop,* ed. J. Kuo, R. Phillips, D. Walker, and H. Kirkman, pp. 213–24. Crawley: University of Western Australia.

Ostrom, Elinor. 1990. *Governing the Commons.* Cambridge: Cambridge University Press.

Pennsylvania Farm Bureau. 2002. "Pennsylvania Agricultural Information." *General Information,* at www.pfb.com/news/aginfo.html (accessed June 5, 2002).

Peters, Guy, and Brian W. Hogwood. 1985. "In Search of the Issue-Attention Cycle." *Journal of Politics* 47: 239–53.

Peters, Guy B. 1999. *American Public Policy: Promise and Performance.* 5th ed. New York: Seven Bridges Press.

Peterson, Paul. 1981. *City Limits.* Chicago: University of Chicago Press.

Potoski, Matthew. 2001. "Clean Air Federalism: Do States Race to the Bottom?" *Public Administration Review* 61, no. 3: 335–42.

Powell, Albert M. 1967. *Historical Information of Maryland Commission of Fisheries with Some Notes on Game.* Unpublished report available from the Maryland Department of Resources Carter Library, Annapolis.

Pritchard, Donald W., and Jerry R. Schubel. 2001. "Human Influence on the Physical Characteristics of the Chesapeake Bay." In *Discovering the Chesapeake: The History of an Ecosystem,* ed. Philip D. Curtin, Grace S. Brush, and George W. Fisher, pp. 60–82. Baltimore: Johns Hopkins University Press.

Rabalais, N. N., R. E. Turner, D. Justic, Q. Dortch, and W. J. Wiseman Jr. 1999. *Characteristics of Hypoxia: Topic 1 Report for the Integrated Assessment of Hypoxia in the Gulf of Mexico (Analysis Series No. 15).* Silver Spring, Md.: National Oceanic and Atmospheric Administration.

Rabe, Barry G. 1997. "Power to the States: The Promise and Pitfalls of Decentralization." In *Environmental Policy in the 1990s: Reform or Reaction?* 2d ed., ed. Norman Vig and Michael E. Kraft, pp. 31–52. Washington, D.C.: Congressional Quarterly Press.

Ringquist, Evan J. 1993. *Environmental Protection at the State Level: Politics and Progress in Controlling Pollution.* Armonk, N.Y.: M. E. Sharpe.

Robinson, Wade L. 1994. *Decisions in Doubt: The Environment and Public Policy.* Hanover, N.H.: University Press of New England.

Rosenbaum, Walter A. 1997. "The EPA at Risk: Conflicts over Institutional Reform." In *Environmental Policy in the 1990s: Toward a New Agenda*, 3d ed., ed. Norman Vig and Michael E. Kraft, pp. 143–68. Washington D.C.: Congressional Quarterly Press.

———. 1998. *Environmental Politics and Policy.* 4th ed. Washington D.C.: Congressional Quarterly Press.

Rudig, Wolfang, ed. 1999. *Environmental Policy Volumes 1–2.* Northampton, Mass.: International Library of Comparative Public Policy.

Sabatier, Paul A. 1988. "An Advocacy Coalition Framework of Public Policy Change and the Role of Policy-Oriented Learning Therein." *Policy Science* 21 (Fall): 129–68.

———. 1991. "Toward Better Theories of the Policy Process." *PS: Political Science and Politics* 24 (June): 147–57.

Sabatier, Paul A., and Hank C. Jenkins-Smith. 1993. *Policy Change and Learning: An Advocacy Coalition Approach.* Boulder, Colo.: Westview.

Sabato, Larry J., Howard R. Ernst, and Bruce A. Larson, eds. 2001. *Dangerous Democracy? The Battle over Ballot Initiatives in America.* Boulder, Colo.: Rowman & Littlefield.

Schlozman, Kay Lehman, and John T. Tierney. 1986. *Organized Interests and American Democracy.* New York: Harper and Row.

Select Committee. 1990. *Final Report: Controlling Nutrient Pollution from Nonpoint Sources in Pennsylvania.* Harrisburg, Pa.: Governor Robert P. Casey's Select Committee on Nonpoint Source Nutrient Management.

Shultz, Mike. 2002. Interview by author. Annapolis, Md., February 15.

Shuyler, L. 1993. "Non-point Source Programs and Progress in the Chesapeake Bay." *Agricultural, Ecosystems and Environment* 46: 217–22.

Simns, Larry. 2001. "Time to Take the Gloves Off." *Waterman's Gazette* (August): 3.

Simpson, Thomas W. 2002. Phone interview by author. Annapolis, Md., August 15.

Smith, David E., M. Leffler, and G. Mackiernan. 1992. *Oxygen Dynamics in the Chesapeake Bay.* College Park: Maryland Sea Grant College.

Sindermann, C. 1989. "Shell Disease Syndrome in Marine Crustaceans." National Oceanic and Atmospheric Administration Technical Memo NMFS-F/NEC-64.

State Game Department of Maryland. 1924a. "Crab Conference by Governors of Virginia and Maryland." *Maryland Conservationist* (Fall): 24.

————. 1924b. "Proposed Conference by Governors of Virginia and Maryland." *Maryland Conservationist* (Fall): 18.

Steadman, David W. 2001. "A Long-Term History of Terrestrial Birds and Mammals in the Chesapeake-Susquehanna Watershed." In *Discovering the Chesapeake: The History of an Ecosystem*, ed. Philip D. Curtin, Grace S. Brush, and George W. Fisher. Baltimore: Johns Hopkins University Press.

Stranko, Denise. 2002. Interview by author. Annapolis, Md., April 19.

Sturgis, R. B., and L. Murray. 1997. "Scaling the Nutrient Inputs to Submersed Plant Communities: Temporal and Spatial Variations." *Marine Ecological Progress Series* 152, nos. 1–3: 89–102.

Swanson, Ann Pesiri. 2001. "Lessons from the Chesapeake Bay Have Applications Elsewhere." *Bay Journal* 11, no. 9, at www.bayjournal.com/01-12/bay.htm (accessed June 19, 2002).

————. 2002. Interview by author. Annapolis, Md., February 27.

Switzer, Jacqueline Vaughn. 1994. *Environmental Politics: Domestic and Global Dimensions.* New York: St. Martin's.

————. 1997. *Green Backlash: The History and Politics of Environmental Opposition in the U.S.* Boulder, Colo.: Rienner.

Switzer, Jacqueline Vaughn, and Gary Bryner. 1998. *Environmental Politics: Domestic and Global Dimensions.* 2d ed. New York: St. Martin's.

Taft, J. L., W. R. Taylor, E. O. Hartwig, and R. Loftus. 1980. "Seasonal Oxygen Depletion in the Chesapeake Bay." *Estuaries* 3: 242–47.

Teitenberg, Tom. 1994. *Environmental Economics and Policy.* New York: Harper Collins.

Thoreau, Henry David. [1843] 1973. "Paradise (To Be) Regained." In *Reform Papers,* ed. Wendell Glick. Princeton, N.J.: Princeton University Press.

————. [1845] 1971. "Walden." In *Henry David Thoreau: Walden,* ed. J. Lyndon Shanley. Princeton, N.J.: Princeton University Press.

Tilghman, Richard A. 2002. Comment made at the Chesapeake Bay Commission Spring Meeting, Gettysburg, Pa., May 10.

Truman, David. 1951. *The Governmental Process.* New York: Knopf.

Trust for Public Land. 2002. *Land Vote 2001: Americans Invest in Parks and Open Spaces.* San Francisco: Trust for Public Land.

Tufte, Edward R. 1978. *Political Control of the Economy.* Princeton, N.J.: Princeton University Press.

U.S. Corps of Engineers. 1973. *Chesapeake Bay Existing Conditions Report.* Baltimore: Army Corps of Engineers (Baltimore District).

————. 1977. *Chesapeake Bay Future Conditions Report.* Baltimore: Army Corps of Engineers (Baltimore District).

————. 1978. *Chesapeake Bay Study: Revised Plan of Study.* Baltimore: Army Corps of Engineers (Baltimore District).

U.S. Department of the Interior. 2000. *Trends and Status of Flow, Nutrients, and Sediments for Selected Nontidal Sites in the Chesapeake Bay Watershed, 1985–1998.* Lemoyne, Pa.: U.S. Geological Survey.

——. 2001. *Trends and Status of Flow, Nutrients, and Sediments for Selected Nontidal Sites in the Chesapeake Bay Watershed, 1985–1999.* New Cumberland, Pa.: U.S. Geological Survey.

Vig, Norman J., and Michael E. Kraft. 1994. *Environmental Policy in the 1990s: Toward a New Agenda.* 2d ed. Washington D.C.: Congressional Quarterly Press.

——. 1997. *Environmental Policy in the 1990s: Reform or Reaction?* 3d ed. Washington D.C.: Congressional Quarterly Press.

Virginia Department of Agriculture. 1997. "County Data Summary." *County Information,* at www.nass.usda.gov/va/bulletin99a.htm (accessed June 5, 2002).

Virginia Marine Resource Commission. 2002. "Historical Highlights of the Virginia Marine Resource Commission." *Highlight Information,* at www.mrc.state.va.us/vmrchist.htm (accessed June 5, 2002).

Wennersten, John R. 1981. *The Oyster Wars of the Chesapeake.* Centreville, Md.: Tidewater.

White, Christopher P. 1989. *Chesapeake Bay Field Guide: Nature of the Estuary.* Centreville, Md.: Tidewater.

Wolman, Able, and John C. Geyer. 1962. *Report on Sanitary Sewers and Waste Water Disposal in the Washington Metropolitan Regions.* Baltimore: Johns Hopkins University Press.

Worster, Donald. 1973. *American Environmentalism: The Formative Period 1860–1915.* New York: Wiley.

Year 2020 Panel. 1988. *Population Growth and Development in the Chesapeake Bay Watershed to the Year 2020.* Final report to the Chesapeake Bay Executive Council, December, Annapolis, Md.

Index

Administrative Executive Legislative Review Committee, 12
aesthetic value. *See* nonuse value of economic resources
agricultural runoff, 47, 60–61, 63, 71–72, 74–75, 86
agriculture: economic value of, 79–81; financial inducements, 80–81, 86, 150; growth, 84, 150; management plans, 47, 74–76, 78, 80, 169n10, 169n23; representation in government, 76–77, 81–83, 117, 144. *See also* best management practices (BMP) for agriculture
air shed, 63
alarmed discovery and euphoric enthusiasm stage, 44–45, 47, 84. *See also* Downs, Anthony
alewife, 19, 23, 24, 24, 162n57
algae, 58, 85, 155, 166n9
algae blooms, 25, 54, 56, 58, 95
Algonquin Indians, 10
Allen Family Foods, 82
Alliance for the Chesapeake Bay, 165n28
American Canoe Association, 132
American Farm Bureau, 8

American Indians, 9, 160n3
American Littoral Society, 132
American shad. *See* shad
animal feed additives, 60–61. *See also* agriculture
animal waste, 2, 53–54, 60–61, 70, 71–72, 75, 80, 154. *See also* agriculture
Annapolis, Md., 14, 90, 107, 108, 119, 137
anoxia, 55
aquaculture techniques, 142–43
aquatic grasses. *See* underwater grasses
Arbor Day, 2
Arctic National Wildlife Refuge (ANWR), 36
Army Corps of Engineers, 2, 13, 14, 147, 161n25
Asian oysters (*Crassostrea ariakensis*), 142–43
Association of Soil Conservation Districts, 82
Atlantic croaker. *See* croaker
Atlantic sturgeon. *See* sturgeon
atmospheric nutrients. *See* nutrients
atmospheric pollution, 25, 148
Audubon Society, 3

nutrient reduction, 58, 149, 150;
financial inducements for, 80–81;
goals, 59, 61, 64, 76, 135, 141,
150–51; innovations, 60–61, 150,
155; management plans, 47,
75–78, 131–32, 151–52, 154–56,
167n22; measurement, 63, 64–67.
See also computer models; farm
plans
Nutrient Reduction Pilot Program,
173n6
nutrients: atmospheric, 25, 54, 64,
59, 72, 148, 152, 153, 167n26;
controllable, 59, 63–66, 75;
effects on habitats, 22, 55–56; and
eutrophication, 54; loading, 47,
58, 60, 71–74, 76, 149, 169n9;
natural cycle, 53–54; nonpoint
source, 54, 62–63, 66, 71, 73, 76,
80, 86, 98, 150–52, 166n6,
169n15, 169n20; point source,
54, 62–63, 72, 73, 98, 150–52,
166n6; reduction, 59, 151, 155;
uncontrollable, 63–66, 72,
167n27. *See also* agriculture;
runoff

oil/gas, as a political contributor, 43
Oil Pollution Act of 1990, 165n38
Olson, Mancur, 40
Osborne, Debbie, 17
Ostrom, Elinor, 33
overfertilization, 54, 56, 71–72. *See
also* agriculture; nutrients, loading
overharvesting, 11–12, 94, 120–21,
142–43. *See also* crab harvesting
oxygen criteria, 56, 57
oxygen depletion, 22, 25, 55–56, 67,
93. *See also* anoxia; hypoxia
oyster police, 109–11
oysters: decline of, 19–20, 70, 91,
94, 101; harvest, 10–11, 19–20,
20; introduced species, 142–43;
management, 12, 16, 58, 89, 105,

109–10, 161n35, 162n44; water
filtration by, 20

parasites, 96
Patapsco River, 93, 168n39, 168n43
Patuxent River, 107–8, 129, 140,
144, 148–49, 156, 168n38,
168n40
Penn, William, 2
Pennsylvania: agricultural
production, 79, 84, 150;
agriculture regulations, 76–78;
cost-sharing programs, 169n21;
environmental spending, 17, 156;
General Assembly, 76–77; nutrient
management, 60, 70, 75, 152–54,
157; results of nutrient
management, 78
Pennsylvania Farm Bureau, 82
Perdue Farms, 82–83, 170n35
pesticides, 24
Peters, Guy, 165n35
Pfiesteria, 47, 56, 58, 77, 85, 86,
140, 155, 166nn9–10
phosphate, and detergents, 44, 46,
60, 62, 70, 150–52
phosphorus, 54, 55, 61, 71–72,
162n61, 166n3, 168nn40–41. *See
also* nutrients
phytoplankton, 53, 54
pocketbook issues, 35. *See also*
economic primacy
Pocomoke, Md., 85
Pocomoke Sound, 90, 100
point source nutrients. *See* nutrients
policy cycle, 44–47; and agriculture,
84–86; and crabs, 122–25. *See
also* disturbance theory
policy funnel. *See* environmental
policy theory
political action committee (PAC),
42–43, 82, 138–39
political contributions, 42–43, 82,
119, 138

About the Author

Howard Ernst lives in Annapolis, Maryland, where he is assistant professor of political science at the United States Naval Academy and senior scholar at the University of Virginia Center for Politics. He earned his Ph.D. from the University of Virginia in 2000. Professor Ernst welcomes your comments and suggestions regarding this book (ernst@usna.edu).